D1207389

SOCIAL CONTROL
IN SLAVE
PLANTATION
SOCIETIES

THE JOHNS HOPKINS UNIVERSITY STUDIES IN HISTORICAL AND POLITICAL SCIENCE

EIGHTY-NINTH SERIES (1971)

1. Social Control in Slave Plantation Societies:
A Comparison of St. Domingue and Cuba
BY GWENDOLYN MIDLO HALL

2. The *Ormée* of Bordeaux:
A Revolution during the *Fronde*
BY SAL ALEXANDER WESTRICH

GWENDOLYN MIDLO HALL

SOCIAL CONTROL IN SLAVE PLANTATION SOCIETIES

A COMPARISON OF ST. DOMINGUE AND CUBA

THE JOHNS HOPKINS PRESS
BALTIMORE AND LONDON

The Johns Hopkins Press, Baltimore, Maryland 21218
The Johns Hopkins Press Ltd., London.

Library of Congress Catalog Card Number 79–163195

ISBN 0-8018-1252-6

TO JAMES WESLEY ODEN, JR., MY BEST TEACHER

CONTENTS

CONTENTS

PREFACE

ALL OF US have to ask ourselves why we spend the little time we have on earth doing what we do. And when we choose such exhausting and painstaking labor as historical research and writing, the only sensible question to ask is, "What is the value of this work?" My belief is that unless history is used as an instrument to deepen our understanding of current pressing social problems and to contribute toward their solution, history is a waste of time; that is, it becomes merely a form of aesthetic enjoyment or a challenging game. This point of view, that history should have a practical application, implies that social phenomena can be known and controlled to a significant extent. Yet this implication appears to conflict with human experience today, for it is obvious that the gap between man's understanding of the physical world and his understanding of society and social forces is rapidly leading to destruction. The basic cause for this gap is philosophic. Social thought still assumes a mechanistic order. Historical concepts are still trapped in a one-sided chain of causality. Social science, while seeking universal patterns, is largely caught up in static abstractions. Those social scientists who attempt to take time and change into account must rely upon the existing historical literature. Social thought is fragmented into "disciplines," with scholars, who are already overspecialized, carving out small areas of expertise and asking safe little questions, the answers to which are at best distorted and at worst insignificant.

This study attempts to transcend the fragmentation of social thought into national history and separate disciplines; the confinement of historical concepts to a mechanistic time sequence on a single plane; the incapacity of the Western mind to perceive others as real, live, active human beings rather than as passive instruments, merely the stage upon which Western man acts. It attempts, by looking at the data in another way and from another place, to perceive a total pattern of interrelationships which can throw new light on the data. The intention of this work is to demonstrate that the apparent meaning of the data is not always the real meaning.

This book is based upon a dissertation submitted to the University of Michigan in partial fulfillment of the requirements for the degree of Doctor of Philosophy. I am indebted to the members of my doctoral committee, William W. Freehling, Arthur P. Mendel, and Eric R. Wolf, for their help and encouragment, and to Charles Gibson, Chairman, for his open-mindedness and for the high standards of scholarship which he and his work inspire. I am grateful to Richard Greenleaf, Rémy Bastien, Ramon Xirau, and Concepción Muedra for encouraging me to continue my studies after a long absence from the academic world. I thank Sidney W. Mintz, David Cohen, and Jack P. Greene for reading the manuscript and offering very helpful suggestions and criticisms. I am particularly indebted to Franklin W. Knight for his very useful criticisms, and for calling the manuscript to the attention of other scholars. I regret that Dr. Knight's book on the slave system of nineteenth-century Cuba was unavailable to me at press time. I am indebted to John Henrik Clarke, Associate Editor of *Freedomways*, and to Hoyt Fuller, Managing Editor of *Negro Digest* (now *Black World*), for their early interest in my work and for publishing my essays. I would like to acknowledge Harry Haywood for the many useful concepts I learned from him during the decade we worked together on theoretical problems of revolutionary black nationalism in the United States. Finally, I am indebted to my neighbors in Bedford-Stuyvesant, Watts, and Detroit for teaching me most of what I know about social reality.

SYMBOLS

A.H.N. Archivo Histórico Nacional, Madrid, Spain.

A.N. Archives Nationales, Paris, France.

Code Noir Edit du Roi, March, 1685. The original, complete text is published in Lucien Peytraud, *L'Esclavage aux antilles françaises avant 1789* (Paris, 1897), pp. 158–66.

C.N.C. *Código negro carolino, formado por la Audiencia de Santo Domingo*, March 14, 1785. Published in *DHFS* (see below), vol. 3, pp. 553–72.

C.N.E. *Códigro negro español,* or *Real Cédula de Su magestad sobre la Educación, Trato, y Ocupaciones de los Esclavos, en Todos sus Dominios de Indias, e Islas Filipinas, Baxo las Reglas que Expresan.* Published in *DHFS* (see below), vol. 3, pp. 643–54.

DHFS Richard Konetzke, ed., *Colección de documentos para la historia de la formación social de Hispanoamérica, 1493–1810* (Madrid, 1962).

Fallos *Colección de los fallos pronunciados por una Sección de la Comisión militar establecida en la ciudad de Matanzas para conocer de la causa de conspiración de la gente de color* (Matanzas, 1844).

Loix M. L. E. Moreau de St.-Méry, *Loix et constitutions des colonies françaises de l'Amérique sous le vent* (Paris, 1784–89).

I

METHODS AND OVERVIEW

THIS STUDY OF comparative slave systems in the Americas is an attempt to apply new methods and new concepts to the field. It is not based on the existing historical literature published in the United States. Although it would be much easier to criticize than to create something better, it is not polemical. For the sake of clarity, nevertheless, we briefly review the existing material and its major conclusions.

Contemporary studies in comparative slavery in the Americas began with Frank Tannenbaum's *Slave and Citizen: The Negro in the Americas.* The main conclusion of this work is that African slavery in Latin America was a relatively mild institution because of the prior experience of the Spanish and Portuguese with slavery which was long established in the Iberian Peninsula. The Spanish and Portuguese were humane in their treatment of slaves. Spanish and Portuguese law and religion (that is, the Roman Catholic Church) protected the slaves. In addition, a legal framework existed for slavery.[1] All of these factors guaranteed its mildness in

---

[1] (New York: Alfred A. Knopf, 1946). Tannenbaum's refers to the Siete Partidas del Rey Alfonso el Sabio. This code, formulated in Toledo, Spain, during the thirteenth century, was according to Tannenbaum, carried over from Roman slave law. But Roman slave law was very harsh. See Arnold A. Sio, "Interpretation of Slavery: The Slave Status in the Americas," *Comparative Studies in Society and History* 7, no. 3 (April, 1965): 289–308. The major influence on the Siete Partidas appears to have been Islamic slave law. See Charles Verlinden, *L'Esclavage dans l'Europe médiévale* (Brugge: De Tempel, 1955), pp. 182–232.

Latin America. The Tannenbaum thesis holds that the slave systems in Spanish and Portuguese America granted the slave the basic rights of a human being and that these systems were open, encouraging emancipation, social mobility, and cultural expression. Furthermore, the universalism of the Roman Catholic Church was an essential factor in safeguarding the rights of the black slaves in Latin America.

The Tannenbaum thesis was developed further by Stanley M. Elkins.[2] Based largely upon the evidence and conclusions of the Tannenbaum study, the Elkins work emphasized the power of the institutions of Church and State in Latin America to substantially modify and humanize the Latin American slave system. Louis Hartz[3] drew even more transcendant conclusions which were based partially on the Tannenbaum study. The Hartz work discusses the extraordinary power of the fragment which broke away from European society in determining the character of new societies. The most recent study, by Herbert S. Klein, neglects nineteenth-century sources for Cuba[4] and assumes that humanitarian progress grew during the nineteenth century.[5]

Comparative history is a challenging pursuit. If it is to avoid becoming a game of logical construction bearing little or no relationship to reality, the historian must avoid assuming too much. Comparative studies that rely heavily upon secondary sources imply a faith in the validity of these sources which is not always justified. The study of comparative slave systems in the Americas is further handicapped by the fact that Afro-American history has been fragmented and treated as part of the history of the various European colonial empires. Because of this fragmentation, the most elementary facts sometimes escape attention.

Certain basic assumptions are made in this study which are not always

[2] Stanley M. Elkins, *Slavery: A Problem in American Institutional and Intellectual Life* (Chicago: University of Chicago Press, 1959).

[3] Louis Hartz, *The Founding of New Societies* (New York: Harcourt, Brace and World, Inc., 1964), pp. 53–58.

[4] Herbert S. Klein, *Slavery in the Americas: A Comparative Study of Virginia and Cuba* (Chicago: University of Chicago Press, 1967). The Archivo Histórico Nacional of Madrid contains most of the archival material in Spain relating to nineteenth-century Cuba. See Arthur F. Corwin, *Spain and the Abolition of Slavery in Cuba, 1817–1886* (Austin and London: University of Texas Press, 1967).

[5] For an excellent critique of the methodology of the Klein study, see comment by Elsa V. Goveia, *Comparative Studies in Society and History* 8, no. 3 (April, 1966): 325–27.

made by historians who compare slave systems in the Americas. These assumptions are:

1. The slave systems were dynamic, not static. The evolution of the slave systems followed the pattern of early development, rise, and decline. This evolution did not take place simultaneously in the various colonies.[6]

2. Progress, in the sense of growing humanitarianism and egalitarianism with the passage of time, is not assumed.

3. The slave systems interacted upon each other. They did not develop in isolation from each other.

4. The Europeans were not omnipotent. Controlling the slaves was a serious problem for the colonists and for the metropolis. Controlling the colonists was a serious problem for the metropolis.

5. Texts of laws published in books are not by themselves accurate indices to the character of the slave system.

6. The African slave trade did not end simply because it was outlawed by international treaty during the early nineteenth century. Continuation of the African slave trade had a serious impact upon the slave systems regularly supplied by this trade.

The comparative study of slave systems in the Americas is a challenge because of the vast amount of material to be handled. It involves dealing with the colonies and activities of five significant European powers: England, France, Portugal, Spain, and Holland. It involves dealing with colonies and nations over three or four centuries. The comparative method, when properly used, is a splendid logical tool which enables us to reduce the variables, pose significant questions, and offer significant answers which might not be made clear within the framework of national history. Unless

---

[6] Studies considering the dynamics of the slave plantation systems include the following: Eric Williams, *Capitalism and Slavery* (Chapel Hill: University of North Carolina Press, 1944); Celso Furtado, *The Economic Growth of Brazil: A Survey from Colonial to Modern Times*, trans. Ricardo W. DeAguiar and Eric C. Drysdale (Berkeley and Los Angeles: University of California Press, 1963); Noel Deerr, *The History of Sugar*, 2 vols. (London: Chapman and Hall, Ltd., 1950); Sidney W. Mintz, "Labor and Sugar in Puerto Rico and Jamaica," *Comparative Studies in Society and History* 7, no. 3 (March, 1959): 273–83; Elsa V. Goveia, "Influence of Religion in the West Indies," *History of Religion in the New World, The Americas* 14, no. 4 (April, 1958): 174–80; Sidney W. Mintz, Introduction to *Sugar and Society in the Caribbean: An Economic History of Cuban Agriculture*, by Ramiro Guerra y Sanchez and translated by Marjory M. Urquidi (New Haven: Yale University Press, 1964).

we set some ground rules, however, it is quite simple to select enough data from this vast amount of material to "prove" any preconceived theory in the mind of the investigator. Unless we select the significant time, place, and circumstance upon which to concentrate and ask the significant questions, we are forced to choose, on the one hand, between the narrow, concrete, and particular upon which to initiate and deepen original research, and, on the other hand, the broadly significant. If we select the latter, we must rely heavily upon secondary sources; in studies of comparative slavery in the Americas, this leads to disaster. While it might be true, as Stanley Elkins maintains, that most of the manuscripts relating to slavery in the United States consist of plantation records which "have already been worked over with great care and thoroughness by eminent scholars,"[7] manuscript materials relating to slave systems *outside* the United States are extremely rich and varied, and practically untouched.

Much of what is cited by North American scholars as fact about Latin American slavery is pure mythology. Polemicists and historians of each of the colonizing powers have claimed that their own slave system was the mildest and most humane, usually with little or no valid basis upon which to make comparisons. At times, antislavery polemicists have indicted the slave system in their own country or colony by comparing it unfavorably with the slave system of another country or colony. Unsubstantiated travelers' accounts and polemical histories are cited and recited as fact, and, with each citation, they gain a greater aura of authenticity.[8]

[7] Elkins, *Slavery*, p. 224.

[8] "An undocumented statement due to Sir Harry Johnson reads, 'Intelligent European travellers in Africa and America during the last half of the eighteenth century recorded the opinions of their own and answers to their questions from negroes which went to show that in the opinion of the negroes themselves the slave-holding nations stood thus in order of merit as regards kind treatment of slaves: the Portuguese first; then the Spaniards, the Danes, the French, English and Dutch.' This statement as adapted by Williamson appears 'Comparative estimates of Spaniards, Frenchmen, British and Dutch as slave-owners united in placing them in that order of merit. Spanish slavery was the mildest, Dutch the harshest, with the British running it close.' As developed by Russel it runs: 'It is rather significant to note that in the West Indies, where Spaniard, French, British and Dutch all shared in the ownership of slaves, the record of mortality statistics, tortures and floggings reveals that the least severity was shown by the Spaniards; then the French; a big gap separated them from the British and Dutch, who were noted for their harshness.'
"The original statement whence the others derive is undocumented and unsupported. Yet it finally appears in the form of being based on official records which are non-existent." Deerr, *History of Sugar*, vol. 2, p. 359 n. The same misinforma-

4

The most essential ground rule for the early stages of investigation is to reduce the variables as much as the material permits. Thus, colonies in a similar state of prosperity should be compared. The major, staple crop had a big impact upon the type of slave system. Wherever possible, colonies that produced the same basic crop should be compared. Because colonies prospered during different periods of time, simultaneity as the crucial factor must be sacrificed.

Before choosing specific colonies to compare at specific times, one should obtain an overall picture of the economic history of the major slaveholding region. It would be useless to generalize from conditions in a colony in which slavery was not an important economic institution compared with a colony in which a flourishing slave plantation economy existed.[9] In fact, to make the comparison as useful as possible, the ideal is to narrow the choice to colonies which were in every respect as similar as possible, except for the major variable: each was colonized by a different European power.

In Brazil and the Caribbean, sugar was the major crop produced by African slave labor. Sugar production required a very large labor force. In sugar colonies, especially in the rural areas, slaves often outnumbered whites ten or twenty to one. This population imbalance tended to produce problems of social relations and social control. At various times and places, each colonizing power had a thriving sugar colony. Because of the ever-shifting economic hegemony among the sugar colonies, one can follow the social impact of the rise and decline of the slave plantation economies. Generalizations made about the impact of institutions of the colonizing powers can best be tested empirically by comparing similar colonies and studying them at various stages of their development. We choose a constant (two flourishing sugar colonies) belonging to two different Euro-

---

tion, as adapted by Tannenbaum, reads: "There were briefly speaking, three slave systems in the Western Hemisphere. The British, American, Dutch, and Danish were at one extreme, and the Spanish and Portuguese at the other. In between these two fell the French. . . . If one were forced to arrange these systems of slavery in order of severity, the Dutch would seem to stand as the hardest, the Portuguese as the mildest, and the French, in between, as having elements of both." Tannenbaum, *Slave and Citizen*, p. 65 n.

[9] See Goveia's comment on Klein's study; also, Gwendolyn Midlo Hall, "Negro Slaves in the Americas," *Freedomways* 4, no. 3 (Summer, 1964): 296–327.

pean powers (a variable). Then we investigate to what extent the slave system took on unique features which can be attributed to the impact of the institutions of the particular colonizing power, and to what extent flourishing sugar colonies tended to take on similar features regardless of which European nation was the colonizer.

The history of the slave plantation system, excluding that of the English mainland colonies, is to a great extent the history of the large-scale, commercial production of sugar for sale on the international market. Two-thirds of the slaves brought to the Americas were brought for the purpose of producing sugar.[10] The slave plantation system, which took root and spread throughout vast regions of the Americas, originated in the South Atlantic Islands off the coast of Africa, where sugar was produced with African slave labor. Sugar production in these islands reached its height during the latter half of the fifteenth century. The system was transmitted to Brazil during the sixteenth century and became the economic basis for Portuguese colonization.[11] Northern Brazil was particularly suited for sugar production. Before the invention of the steam engine, water-driven mills were the most productive source of power, and water transport of the bulky sugar stalks was the most easy and economical method of transport. In the absence of water power, the much less productive horse-powered mills were used.[12] The northern coast of Brazil was full of small rivers flowing through adjacent valleys and then to the sea. The rivers drove the sugar mills and served as arteries of trade and transport. Brazil's proximity to Africa was an advantage, because the voyage of the slave ships was shorter than that to other areas of the Americas.[13]

The Portuguese had learned the technical and organizational secrets of sugar production from their experience on the South Atlantic Islands. But the Dutch played the essential role of refining and marketing the produce of the early sugar industry of Brazil. Crude sugar produced in Brazil was

[10] Deerr, *History of Sugar.*

[11] Gilberto Freyre, *The Masters and the Slaves* (New York: Alfred A. Knopf, 1947), p. 266; Furtado, *Growth of Brazil*, pp. 1–2.

[12] Fernando Ortiz, *Cuban Counterpoint: Tobacco and Sugar*, trans. Harriet de Onís (New York: Alfred A. Knopf, 1947), p. 266.

[13] Johan Nieuhoff, *Voyages and Travels into Brazil and the East Indies, 1643*, extracted from Awsham Churchill, *A Collection of Voyages and Travels*, vol. 2 (London, 1704), p. 31.

shipped to Lisbon, and from there to Antwerp and Amsterdam. Antwerp was soon pushed out of competition, and Amsterdam became the major refining center from which the finished product was distributed throughout Europe. The Dutch largely financed the early Brazilian sugar industry and were in control of trade and transport. The early Brazilian sugar industry was an integral part of the Dutch economy.[14]

Just as the Dutch, to a great extent, created the Brazilian sugar industry, the Dutch also destroyed it. This development was a phase of the Dutch war for independence against Spain (1580–1640). The Spanish and Portuguese crowns were united, and the Dutch occupied North Brazil as part of the military operations of the war. During this period, the Dutch learned every angle, technical and organizational, of sugar production. When they were driven from Brazil, they created a competitive sugar industry on the French and British Caribbean islands. The Dutch provided expensive sugar mill equipment and slaves on credit. They brought British and French settlers to North Brazil to learn the techniques and organization of sugar production first hand. They provided transport and marketing facilities.

Following Portuguese independence from Spain, Philip IV of Spain revoked the Portuguese asiento which had given Portugal exclusive rights to engage in the African slave trade. The Dutch thereafter took over the African slave trade and secured a virtual monopoly. The competitive sugar industry grew rapidly in the Caribbean, and the Brazilian industry was ruined. The price of sugar declined 50 percent during the second half of the seventeenth century. Brazilian production dropped 50 percent from the height it had reached in 1650; this reduced the income of the Brazilian sugar industry to one-fourth of its former level.[15]

The penetration into the Caribbean by the North Atlantic powers during the seventeenth century was basically a military operation. England

[14] Furtado, *Growth of Brazil*, pp. 8, 9.

[15] Arthur P. Newton, *The European Nations in the West Indies: 1493–1688* (London: A. and C. Black, Ltd., 1939), pp. 40–45; Furtado, *Growth of Brazil*, p. 17. For contemporary accounts of the Dutch role in initiating and promoting the sugar industry in the British West Indies, see Richard Ligon, *A True and Exact History of the Island of Barbados* (London, 1757), pp. 52, 85. For the Dutch role in the French West Indies, see Jean-Baptiste Dutertre, *Histoire générale des antilles habitées par les français*, 4 vols. (Paris, 1667–71), 2:515.

and France considered their Caribbean colonies essentially as beachheads in their ambitions to seize the coveted precious-metal–producing colonies on the Spanish American mainland.[16] They did not welcome the growth of the sugar industry in their Caribbean colonies, for this conflicted with their original purposes in founding these colonies. Britain and France wanted settlement colonies, and favored small farms to attract settlers. They encouraged the production of such crops as cotton, indigo, coffee, and especially tobacco which could be raised on small farms. Their basic objective was to control islands populated with European settlers who could constitute a permanent militia, setting up bridgeheads against the Spanish Empire. Desperate means were used to obtain settlers, including forced transport of convicts and vagrants, the kidnapping of men, women, and children, and the forced transport of prisoners taken during the Irish Rebellion. Since the enclosure system had forced many British rural laborers out of agriculture, British settlers were more available than either French or Spanish settlers.[17]

Britain temporarily lost direction of her Caribbean colonies during the Glorious Revolution and the civil war that followed. Economic conditions in the Caribbean allowed the Dutch to use the British and French islands for their own purposes. By the middle of the seventeenth century, Barbados tobacco had been forced off the market by the superior Virginia product. Attempts at commercial production of cotton and indigo had failed. The commercial production of sugar, engineered by the Dutch, was immediately successful. Much to the chagrin of Britain and France, the slave population rapidly increased, while the European population rapidly declined, subverting the original strategic purpose of the colonies. Efforts by British and French colonial authorities to reverse the process failed.[18]

Strategic considerations remained paramount in French Caribbean policy throughout the late seventeenth century. A law provided that settlers must have an equal number of *engagés* (indentured servants) and slaves, under penalty of confiscation of the excess slaves.[19] Because French settlers were scarce, emacipation of slaves was encouraged, freedmen were given full

---

[16] Furtado, *Growth of Brazil*, pp. 4, 5.
[17] *Ibid.*, pp. 21–23.
[18] Newton, *European Nations*, pp. 195–97; Furtado, *Growth of Brazil*, pp. 27–30.
[19] *Loix*, Ordonnance du Roi, May 2, 1686.

French citizenship rights, regardless of their place of birth, and marriage between white masters and their slave concubines was encouraged.

In the long run, rivalry between Britain and France defeated the ambitions of *both* powers to conquer the Spanish mainland colonies. They soon discovered, however, that black gold was more valuable than yellow.[20] By the early eighteenth century, Britain and France had usurped the role of the Dutch as financiers, marketers, transporters, refiners, and suppliers of slaves for their Caribbean colonies. The British and French West Indies became colonies of economic exploitation rather than strategic colonies.

By the 1740s, St. Domingue became the most important overseas possession of France because of both the riches which she derived from the colony and the influence it exerted on French commerce.[21] The French one-third of the Island of Hispaniola was well equipped for sugar production. It had abundant water power and fertile land. The economic policies of the French Bourbons encouraged the coffee, banana, and indigo industries, as well as the sugar industry. St. Domingue became a fabulously wealthy colony in which, by 1789, nearly two-thirds of France's foreign commercial interests were centered. During prosperous years, more than 700 ocean-going vessels, employing as many as 80,000 seamen, visited her ports.[22] Colonial administration was highly centralized, and French law and policy were concrete and specific. The documents clearly explain the motives for the measures taken. St. Domingue has been well researched and studied, because of its importance to France. It was a colony torn by conflicts which finally exploded in the Haitian Revolution, making it, in a sense, a classic slave colony in which to study the problem of social control.[23]

The slave plantation system in the Spanish colonies, particularly in Cuba, was not significant until the nineteenth century. Sugar production was severely limited by the Spanish Crown. The Spanish colonies were

---

[20] Furtado, *Growth of Brazil*, p. 19.

[21] M. L. E. Moreau de Saint-Méry, *Description topographique, physique, civile, politique, et historique de la partie française de l'isle St. Domingue*, 4 vols. (Paris: Librarie Larose, 1958), 1:i-viii.

[22] James G. Leyburn, *The Haitian People* (New Haven: Yale University Press, 1941), p. 19.

[23] The best study of the Haitian Revolution is C. L. R. James, *The Black Jacobins*, 2d ed. rev. (New York: Vintage Books, 1963). For the internal conflicts leading to the revolution, see Gaston-Martin, *Histoire de l'esclavage dans les colonies françaises* (Paris: Presses Universitaires de France, 1948), pp. 172–77.

not allowed to export sugar, since production was for local consumption only. This measure, which prevented colonial competition on the Spanish domestic market, was taken to protect the sugar industry of Andalusia.[24] African slaves were primarily introduced into the Spanish colonies not to further the commercial production of sugar, but to replace the Indian population where it had died out in the Caribbean colonies and to prevent the complete extermination of the Indians on the mainland. Thus, in the Viceroyalty of New Spain during the sixteenth century, Indians could not work in the mines, as pearl divers, or on sugar plantations. This work was to be carried out by African slaves who, while proving as mortal as the Indians, could be replaced by the African slave trade without disrupting the native Indian society.[25]

Once Mexico had been discovered and conquered, Cuba quickly lost its importance. During the exodus to Mexico from 1518 to 1522, the Spanish Caribbean Islands became mere ports of call.[26] Cuba offered few financial attractions for settlers, and few African slaves were brought there. The tendency was to desert the island entirely. In 1526, Spanish settlers were forbidden to leave Cuba under penalty of death.[27] The population, especially the black population, increased very slowly.[28]

Cuba had neither strategic nor administrative importance during the sixteenth and the first half of the seventeenth centuries. Santo Domingo was the administrative center of the Spanish Caribbean. When the North Atlantic powers began to penetrate, settle, and stake out territorial claims during the seventeenth century, the strategic colonization of Cuba got underway, and the population began to increase very slowly. When Spain lost Jamaica to Britain in 1655, a nucleus of Spanish colonists came to Cuba from that colony.[29]

Cuba stretched out like a shield over the trade routes from Spain's rich continental colonies, and Spanish treasure ships filled with gold and silver

[24] Furtado, *Growth of Brazil*, p. 14 n; Fernando B. Sandoval, *La industria del azúcar en Nueva España* (Mexico: U.N.A. de México, Instituto de Historia, 1951).

[25] Silvio Zavala, "Los trabajadores antillanos en el siglo XVI," *Revista de Historia de América* 1, no. 3 (September, 1938): 60–89.

[26] Newton, *European Nations*, pp. 40–45.

[27] Fernando Ortiz, *La hampa afro-cubana: Los negros esclavos* (Havana: Ruiz y Cᵃ, 1916), pp. 4, 69, 70.

[28] *Ibid.*, pp. 21, 22.

[29] *Ibid.*, pp. 4, 5.

from Mexican and Peruvian mines stopped at Havana. Designated an area of lesser economic significance, Cuba was settled for purposes of supply and defense. During this strategic period of Cuban colonization, the importance of Havana was dependent upon its value as a center of government and defense rather than as a commercial port for the products of the island.[30] The possibilities of plantation agriculture were sacrificed to defense from encroachments by the North Atlantic powers. Defense of the island was incompatible with a large slave population. The Caribbean was terrorized by colonies of escaped slaves who settled in remote areas, raided settlements for supplies, drove off cattle and slaves, and cooperated with the Indians as well as with the North Atlantic pirates and filibusters.[31] Slave rebellions in the Spanish Antilles were constant and dated from the earliest years of colonization. Strategic considerations remained paramount in Cuba until the late eighteenth century. It was not until the Bourbon Reform period under Charles III that the commercial possibilities of plantation agriculture in the Spanish Antilles were seriously explored and encouraged.

St. Domingue exerted a decisive influence on the Cuban slave system. The example of the prosperous neighboring French colony inspired the Spanish Bourbons to emulate French free trade policies. As a result of the enlightenment economic policies instituted under Charles III, free trade in slaves was promulgated, Havana was opened up to trade within the Empire, and economic activity was greatly stimulated in the Spanish Caribbean. An attempt was made to formulate a Spanish slave code using the French Code Noir as a model.[32]

The Haitian Revolution of the 1790s removed the sugar production of St. Domingue from the world market. The American Revolution opened up new possibilities for trade with the United States. The industrial revolution produced steam-powered sugar mills and railroads, minimizing the

---

[30] Newton, *European Nations*, pp. 40–45.

[31] Carter G. Woodson, *The Negro in Our History* (Washington, D.C.: The Associated Publishers, Inc., 1947), p. 79.

[32] Raúl Carranca y Trujillo, "El estatuo jurídico de los esclavos en las postrimerías de la colonización español," *Revista de Historia de América* 1, no. 3 (September, 1938): 20–60; Javier Malagón, "Un documento del siglo XVIII para la historia de la esclavitud en las Antillas," *Imago Mundi* 1, no. 9 (September, 1955): 38–56.

problem of lack of water power and waterways for transportation in Cuba. The success of the independence movements in the Spanish mainland colonies obviated Cuba's former role as a strategic colony. During the nineteenth century, Cuba emerged from economic decline, and at last became a colony whose economic resources, based mainly on the sugar monoculture, were exploited by the metropolis. It is not until the nineteenth century that we can speak of a slave plantation system in Cuba.[33]

In this study, we compare eighteenth-century St. Domingue with nineteenth-century Cuba and examine the evolution of significant aspects of both societies from the pre-plantation period through the emergence of the colonies as the leading suppliers of sugar for the world market.

[33] C. M. Macinnes, *England and Slavery* (Bristol: J. W. Arrowsmith, Ltd., 1934), pp. 104, 105.

II

THE PROBLEM OF THE SURVIVAL
OF THE SLAVE POPULATION

THE SLAVE POPULATION in the sugar colonies did not reproduce itself naturally. Its survival depended upon being constantly renewed by the African slave trade. High mortality and low reproduction rates were characteristic of all the sugar colonies, regardless of the colonizing power.

Customs house returns of the British Antilles reveal that between 1680 and 1786, 2,130,000 slaves were brought from the African coast. By the early nineteenth century, these colonies contained only about 700,000 blacks and mulattoes, free and slave.[1] These figures apparently do not take into account the reexport of slaves, a considerable number since the British West Indies served as seasoning stations where slaves coming from Africa were socialized into the system and then reexported to other colonies. Nevertheless, studies which take into account the reexport figures still show an annual natural decrease in Jamaica, ranging between 1.5 percent and 3.7 percent during the eighteenth century.[2] Mortality among slaves working on sugar estates was especially high. Bookkeeping records of a late

[1] Alexander von Humboldt, *The Island of Cuba* (New York: Derby and Jackson, 1856), p. 222 n.
[2] Orlando Patterson, *The Sociology of Slavery: An Analysis of the Origin, Development, and Structure of Negro Slave Society in Jamaica* (New York: Humanities Press, 1969), p. 97.

eighteenth-century sugar estate in Jamaica allowed 750 pounds for a yearly decrease of 6 percent in the slave stock.[3]

Brazil was a great consumer of slaves. Throughout the history of slavery in Brazil, the slave population showed a constantly diminishing life span. Nothing was successfully done to reverse the process.[4] Conditions in the nineteenth century were particularly severe. At the beginning of the century, for example, both Brazil and the United States had one million slaves. By the outbreak of the Civil War in the United States, Brazil had only about one and a half million slaves while the United States had four million, in spite of the fact that about a million additional slaves were imported into Brazil and only about a quarter million imported into the United States during this period. Overwork and precarious living conditions were the major factors in the high mortality rate in Brazil.[5] The get-rich-quick mentality of Brazilian coffee planters during the nineteenth century soon led to a depletion of their slave supply. One coffee planter who had bought a hundred slaves calculated that at the end of three years, twenty-five would be left. All the others would have died or run away.[6]

The mortality rate among slaves in St. Domingue was extremely high. Between 1680 and 1777, more than 800,000 African slaves were brought to the colony. The slave population was calculated to be 290,000 during the 1770s. The reexport rate from St. Domingue was not significant.[7] Toward the end of the colonial period, 15,000 slaves per year were imported, but the population grew very slowly. Overwork was a major factor in the high mortality rate.[8] A study of the operation of a sugar estate in late eighteenth-century St. Domingue reveals that the entire work force, consisting of 150 slaves, had to be renewed between 1765 and 1778.[9]

[3] Noel Deerr, *The History of Sugar*, 2 vols. (London: Chapman and Hall, Ltd., 1950), 2:334.

[4] Celso Furtado, *The Economic Growth of Brazil: A Survey from Colonial to Modern Times*, trans. Ricardo W. DeAguiar and Eric C. Drysdale (Berkeley and Los Angeles: University of California Press, 1963), p. 51.

[5] *Ibid.*, p. 128.

[6] Gilberto Freyre, *The Mansions and the Shanties* (New York: Alfred A. Knopf, 1963), pp. 130, 131.

[7] Hilliard d'Auberteuil, *Considerations sur l'etat présent de la colonie française de St. Domingue*, 2 vols. (Paris, 1776–77), 2:62, 63.

[8] Gaston-Martin, *Histoire de l'esclavage dans les colonies françaises* (Paris: Presses Universitaires de France, 1948), pp. 124, 125.

[9] Gabriel Debien, *Plantations et esclaves à St. Domingue* (Dakar: Publications de la Section d'Histoire, Université de Dakar, 1962), pp. 50, 51.

Convincing evidence indicates that the mortality rate among slaves on Cuban sugar estates reached unprecedented heights during the nineteenth century, in spite of the fact that Alexander von Humboldt compared the Cuban record favorably with that of the British West Indies. Humboldt calculated that a total of 413,500 slaves had been introduced into Cuba from Africa by 1825. In that year, the blacks, free and slave, numbered 320,000 and the mulattoes numbered 70,000, totaling 390,000. If we consider that there were 100,000 free blacks in Cuba in 1825, who, because of the strategic role Cuba played, had enjoyed relatively good conditions, it is evident that these figures are not very enlightening about the mortality rate among slaves. Humboldt reported that some persons who were well informed about the "old system on the plantations believe that in the present state of things, the number of slaves would diminish 5 percent annually if the contraband traffic should entirely cease." [10] Another contemporary observer indicated a 10 percent annual loss by death on Cuban sugar estates, but claimed a marked improvement with the introduction of the steam engine and the example set by foreigners of milder treatment of slaves. [11] A recent study of estate records from the mid-nineteenth century indicates an annual death rate ranging from 4 percent to 10 percent of the work force, and a 10 percent annual drop in the work force on large sugar estates. [12]

High mortality is clearly revealed by the fact that production was quickly and sharply curtailed because of a labor shortage when the supply of slaves was not regularly replenished. An investigation into the causes for the decadence of the Cuban sugar industry during the Napoleonic Wars is revealing. The Marquis de Casa-Peñalver had lost sixty slaves from his three sugar mills in two years and did not want to replace them because his possessions did not return a profit. The Marquis de Monte-Hermoso reported that his four sugar mills, then in a state of decadence, had formerly produced 5,000 boxes of sugar. During the past five years he had bought only ten slaves in payment of a debt, "although he needed 250 Negroes more to maintain the said sugar estates in an ordinary state

[10] Humboldt, *Island of Cuba*, p. 229.

[11] J. G. F. Wurdemann, *Notes on Cuba* (Boston: James Monroe and Co., 1844), pp. 153–54.

[12] Manuel Moreno Fraginals, *El ingenio: El complejo económico social cubano del azucar* (Havana: Comisión Nacional Cubana de la UNESCO, 1964), pp. 51, 155.

of culture."[13] In the late 1830s, an investigation of the sugar estate of the Conde de O'Reilly, an absentee owner who lived in Havana, revealed that production was declining because of a labor shortage. The Conde was not selling his slaves, but since he was in debt, he was not buying new ones.[14] It is evident from these concrete examples that some sugar estates could not maintain their normal level of production without a constant renewal of their work force.

MORTALITY AND OVERWORK

The rapid using up of the work force was the rule rather than the exception, because the colonial officials and the metropolis were always greatly concerned that the work force on the sugar estates would disappear once the illegal African slave trade ended in practice as well as in law. Leopoldo O'Donnell, Captain-General of Cuba during the mid-1840s, after being instructed to find ways to reduce mortality among plantation slaves, laid great emphasis upon the impact of overwork.

. . . it is most important to reduce the number of work hours on the sugar plantations to rational proportions [*a un término racional*] to bring about the conservation of the robustness and life of the slaves for a longer time. These hours, which presently are distributed in a way that hardly leaves the operator the time necessary for food and for rest, should be arranged in a way that would allow prudent rest capable of avoiding his precipitous ruin.[15]

Overwork was undoubtedly a major factor in the high mortality rate among slaves in sugar colonies. The intensity of the labor demanded by sugar production was certainly crucial. Sugar stalks were heavy and bulky. The harvest season lasted from five to six months of the year. The cane had to be ground as soon as it was cut or the yield of juice would shrink, ferment, and spoil. The workers who did the cutting could not be the same as those who did the grinding of the stalks and the boiling of the syrup.

[13] *Recueil de diverses pièces et des discussions qui ont eu lieu aux Cortès générales sur l'abolition de la traite et de l'esclavage des Nègres* (Paris, 1814), p. 132. This and subsequent translations from Spanish and French are my own, unless otherwise noted.

[14] Richard R. Madden, *The Island of Cuba* (London, 1853), pp. 167–68.

[15] A.H.N. Ultramar, Legajo 4655, Expediente 181, Raza Blanca y de Color, Carta de O'Donnell al Sec. de Estado, February 15, 1845; Informe de la Sección de Ultramar del Consejo Real, December 22, 1846.

The operations of cutting, hauling, grinding, clarification, filtration, evaporation, and crystalization had to be carried out in that order, without interruption, simultaneously, and at top speed. Although the grinding season lasted for months, the conversion of each stalk into sugar had to be completed within a few hours.[16] Because each plantation was a self-contained unit, and a limited supply of floating labor was available during the grinding season, excessive hours, including night and Sunday work, were an absolute necessity.[17] Slave labor was not spared, however, even outside of crop time. Slave manpower has been compared to plant equipment. The purchase price of the slave was the investment, and the maintenance of the slave was a fixed cost that had to be paid whether or not the slave was working. Just as the lost utilization of a machine that has to be discarded after a fixed number of years cannot be recovered, a lost hour of slave labor, economically speaking, was a waste, because the slave's labor was being paid for whether he worked or not. Out of crop season, the sugar plantation slaves did construction work, opened up new lands, and did fencing, ditching, other local improvements, and personal services.[18] But labor during the grinding season was particularly long and hard. Estimates from various sugar colonies in the Americas are on the order of eighteen to twenty hours a day. A description of the spell system enforced on estates in the British West Indies during the 1830s indicates one type of operation. All able-bodied workers were divided into two spells on small estates and three spells on large ones. Each spell was divided into two divisions. The first division worked from 8 p.m. to midnight; the second division from midnight to 6 p.m. For the first division, this labor was, of course, in addition to a full day's work in the fields, which began at 5 a.m. Thus each division worked from 5 a.m. to midnight one day, and from midnight until 6 p.m. the following day, alternating with each other on the night shift so that operations were uninterrupted.[19]

The workday during the grinding season on sugar estates in mid-nineteenth-century Cuba reached twenty hours. A traveler during the 1840s

---

[16] Ferando Ortiz, *Cuban Counterpoint: Tobacco and Sugar*, trans. Harriet de Onís (New York: Alfred A. Knopf, 1947), p. 33.

[17] Deerr, *History of Sugar*, vol. 2, pp. 354–55.

[18] Furtado, *Economic Growth of Brazil*, p. 53.

[19] Deerr, *History of Sugar*, vol. 2, pp. 354–55. Testimony before a Parliamentary Commission in 1832, cited therein.

reported the incessant sound of the whip. "Indeed, it was necessary to keep the poor wretches awake." [20] Toward the end of the grinding season, even the oxen were reduced to "mere skeletons, many of them dying from over-labor; the negroes are allowed but five hours sleep." [21] Other reports indicate that four hours sleep was considered sufficient for a slave, and that twenty hours a day for five to seven months out of the year was the normal working day. Even on one well-run estate, which had a humane manager who had been with the family for thirty years, only three to four hours sleep was allowed during the grinding season. The manager explained apologetically that the work could not be carried on with less labor. When the manager of another estate was asked whether the slaves' lives were shortened by lack of sleep during crop time, he replied "without doubt [sin duda]." [22] Keeping the slaves constantly occupied was also justified as a means of keeping them out of trouble. Cuban planters were amazed when informed of the amount of leisure that slaves in the United States enjoyed after their daily tasks were finished. They could not understand how the slaves remained disciplined with so much time on their hands. [23]

The nature of the crop was not, however, the only factor determining the intensity of labor. Fluctuations in the market for various crops encouraged planters to get in as big a crop as possible while prices were high. Slaves in the tobacco industry in the French West Indies during the seventeenth century were worked from early morning through most of the night and were allowed only three or four hours sleep. They often fell asleep standing up and were struck if they were found sleeping. From the time they were twelve years old, women and children were worked with the same intensity. The burden was lightened for women during the seventh or eighth month of pregnancy. [24] While labor on the coffee estates in mid-nineteenth-century Cuba was less intense (the workday was fifteen to sixteen hours) and the mortality rate was lower, [25] the coffee industry in Brazil maintained an extremely intense labor regime. With inadequate

[20] *Ibid.*, vol. 2, p. 359.
[21] Wurdemann, *Notes on Cuba*, pp. 153–54.
[22] Madden, *Island of Cuba*, pp. 167–68.
[23] Wurdemann, *Notes on Cuba*, p. 258.
[24] Jean-Baptiste Dutertre, *Histoire générale des antilles habitées par les françois*, 4 vols. (Paris, 1667–71), 2:523.
[25] David Turnbull, *Travels in the West Indies* (London, 1840), p. 294.

food, slaves worked from 3 a.m. until 9 or 10 p.m. Even during the rainy season, slaves had to pick coffee at night. One coffee planter calculated upon using a slave no longer than a year, "longer than which few could survive, but that he got enough work out of him not only to repay his initial investment, but even to show a good profit!"[26] What is unique about sugar production, however, is that even with the best intentions and the most humane management, the nature of the crop itself and the process involved in producing raw sugar, in the absence of an elastic labor supply, made intense utilization of the work force inevitable during the extended grinding season.

Moreno Fraginals, who has carefully researched nineteenth-century Cuban sugar estate records, concluded that conditions were the most barbaric in the entire world during certain periods of the last century. Contrary to the belief of some observers that mechanization of the sugar industry would improve working conditions for the slaves, the opposite result was produced. While the sugar mill was mechanized and railroads were used for transportation, field work remained unmechanized. Bottlenecks resulted, more slaves were needed, the length of the workday and the intensity of labor were increased. Little sentimentality crept into the calculations of management. Treatment of slaves was determined by the volume of manpower available, the price of the slave, techniques of production, and market conditions. Cuban estates operated under a highly rationalized system of time control. The slave's possibilities for survival depended upon the concepts of economy held by management at a particular time. If high productivity was chosen at the expense of a high mortality rate, slaves died in mass.[27]

Colonial authorities in Madrid, discussing the impact of ending the African slave trade, indicated that in 1847 there were 80,000 slaves working on the 1,240 sugar estates of Cuba, and that 8,000 additional slaves were needed each year to "maintain the existing number of slaves on the sugar estates."[28] Evidence of an unusually high mortality rate on sugar

---

[26] Freyre, *The Mansions and the Shanties*, p. 131. See also Stanley J. Stein, *Vassouras: A Brazilian Coffee County, 1850–1900* (Cambridge, Mass.: Harvard University Press, 1957).

[27] Moreno Fraginals, *El ingenio*, pp. 155–62.

[28] A.H.N. Ultramar, Raza Blanca y de Color.

estates in mid-nineteenth-century Cuba might suggest an upward revision in the figures calculated for the slave trade to Cuba in Philip D. Curtin's recent work.[29]

SUICIDE AMONG SLAVES

From the earliest days of the African slave trade, suicide was widely reported among the slaves. Various methods were used. Slavers noted death from a state described as *fixed melancholy.* The slaves lost their desire to live, stopped eating or drinking, and died. Mass and individual drownings were common.[30] Slaves killed themselves by suffocation with their own tongues. Moreau de St.-Méry commented upon "the frivolity of the motives which bring them to employ this means."[31] Mass hangings were a common means employed, especially among the Ebo. A high suicide rate among certain tribes was attributed to their belief in the transmigration of souls. They believed that when they died they returned to their own country and to family and friends once again.[32] The Ebo reputation for suicide extended throughout the hemisphere, including the English mainland colonies. Henry Laurens, a leading commission merchant in Charleston, South Carolina, who later became president of the Continental Congress, wrote in 1757 that he could not sell a newly arrived shipment of "Abous" because they were known to commit suicide.[33] In St. Domingue, it often happened that all the Ebos of a plantation would form the project of hanging themselves in order to return to their own country. Many colonists hestiated to buy them, but others preferred them because they were very attached to each other and "the newly arrived find help, care, and example from those who have come before them."[34] The slaves

---

[29] *The Atlantic Slave Trade: A Census* (Madison: University of Wisconsin Press, 1969), pp. 40–42.

[30] Daniel Pratt Mannix in collaboration with Malcolm Cowley, *Black Cargoes: A History of the Atlantic Slave Trade* (New York: Viking Press, 1962), pp. 19, 120; Johan Nieuhoff, *Voyages and Travels into Brazil and the East Indies, 1643,* extracted from Awsham Churchill, *A Collection of Voyages and Travels,* vol. 2 (London, 1704), p. 31.

[31] M. L. E. Moreau de St.-Méry, *Description topographique, physique, civile, politique, et historique de la partie française de l'Isle Saint-Domingue,* 4 vols. (Philadelphia, 1797), 1:78.

[32] Mannix and Cowley, *Black Cargoes,* p. 118.

[33] *Ibid.,* p. 19.

[34] Moreau de St.-Méry, *Description de l'isle St. Domingue,* vol. 1, p. 51.

of St. Domingue gained a reputation for being fearless and contemptuous of death. "The greatest dangers, and even death, do not frighten the Negroes. They are more courageous than men subjected to slavery should be. They appear insensible amidst torture, and are inclined to suicide." [35]

Suicide among slaves on Cuban estates reached such proportions during the 1840s that colonial officials carried out an investigation to determine how to conserve these "useful hands [*utiles brazos*]." They hoped to prevent the frequent suicides "which the men of color allow themselves to be dragged down to [*a que se dejan arrastrar los hombres de color*], who today we try to protect from all accidents [*a quienes hoy procura guardarse de todo accidente*]." [36] During the course of this investigation, the Intendant of Cuba reported mass hangings on his own estates.

. . . for committing suicide, they never adopt other means except hanging themselves from trees or in their huts. And in doing so, they put on all their clothes, put unconsumed food in their hats, and even bring to the place where they are to die the animals which belong to them, the better to return well supplied to their native land where they believe they go body and soul. . . .

To discourage suicide, some administrators of the sugar estates in former times had burned the corpses of the victims in the presence of those companions who seemed to be most inclined to follow their example. But this device did not always work. Their companions sometimes hanged themselves from the same tree. [37]

The figures cited during the course of that investigation were minimal, because many suicides were concealed to avoid costly investigations which would have to be paid for by the master. The Bishop of Havana was informed by his parish priests that there were many more suicides than those reported to the authorities. [38] Official records of the suicides actually re-

---

[35] Hilliard d'Auberteuil, *Considerations sur l'état*, vol. 1, p. 141.

[36] A.H.N. Ultramar, Legajo 4655, No. 816, Testimonios del expediente formado par averiguar las causes que influyen en el frecuente suicidio de los esclavos, Carta de O'Donnell al Sec. de Estado, September 18, 1847.

[37] *Ibid.*, Informe del Conde de Villanueva, Havana, June 30, 1847.

[38] *Ibid.*, Informe de Exmo. Sor. Francisco Obispo de la Habana, March 6, 1847. Forwarded by the Captain-General to the *Regente de la Audiencia Pretorial de la Habana*, March 16, 1847.

Wurdemann gave an interesting account of the consequences of a suicide which he witnessed in mid-nineteenth-century Cuba. A Cuban doctor left a suicide note

ported to the authorities revealed that from April, 1839 through November, 1846, 1,337 suicides were investigated. Among these were 115 whites, 51 free colored, and 1,171 slaves. Thus slaves comprised 86.7 percent, whites 8.7 percent, and free colored 3.9 percent of the suicides investigated. The fiscal took note that many suicides were concealed to avoid investigation, so that these were minimal figures.[39] He concluded that suicide "is not an inherent propensity in the colored race, since we see that among the whites and the free colored, there are many more of the former than of the latter who commit suicide. It is therefore necessary to seek in slavery the cause of suicide of the Negroes." His computation over the preceding six years, since 1840, was as follows:

5 per 10,000 among the white, or	0.8 percent
9 per 10,000 among the free colored, or	1.5 percent
36 per 10,00 among the slaves, or	6.1 percent

Absolute figures were broken down into two-year periods:

	White	Free Colored	Slave
1840–41	38	1	285
1842–43	39	17	449
1844–45	43	25	303

with the mayoral of the estate which Wurdemann was visiting, then drove off the estate and killed himself. Although the suicide note absolved the mayoral of any guilt in connection with the doctor's death, the mayoral concealed the note from the public officer so that he would not be brought within the clutches of the law. Although he had a clear alibi, not having left the estate after dinner, he was so upset at the risk he ran of being suspected and arrested that he suffered from insomnia for many nights. "Had the suicide been committed on a private estate, it would have been charged with all the investigations relating to it, amounting to several hundred dollars, which it appears the poor doctor had not lost sight of when selecting the place of his self-murder." Wurdemann cited another incident involving the attempted suicide of a United States citizen, an indigent carpenter who was put into stocks and later released after the intervention of the United States consul. "But the attendant physicians had not received their fees; and learning that the gentleman at whose house the man boarded had given him a dose of oil the evening previous to his committing the deed, they indicted him for practicing without a license, affirming that the oil had caused the suicidal mania. It was only by a compromise that the gentleman escaped from an expensive lawsuit." Wurdemann, *Notes on Cuba*, pp. 127–28.

[39] A.H.N. Ultramar, Testimonios . . . para averiguar . . . suicidio de los esclavos, Informe de Regino Martin, October 27, 1846.

The fiscal concluded that suicide rose "little among the whites, some among the free colored, but among the slaves, comparing the first two-year period with the second and the third, the progress of suicide which is observed is alarming." Suicide was almost seven times more frequent among slaves than among whites; almost six times more frequent among slaves than among free colored, "and among slaves it has increased by 50 percent, comparing the years 1840–41 with those of 1844–45, while in the other classes, no more, perhaps, than what can be expected from the population increase." While these figures are undoubtedly distorted because of the concealment of suicides, the distortion would probably lie in minimizing the rate among slaves, since the isolation of the rural estates and the power of the masters would facilitate concealment.

While suicide among slaves during 1843 and 1844 was extraordinarily high because of the "rigor and severity with which the conspiracies among the Negroes were put down," the Consejo de Ministros' expectation that suicide should "diminish with the end of the slave trade, since suicides are most frequent among slaves recently arrived from Africa"[40] was not realized. Suicide continued to assume epidemic proportions. The only significant change was that Chinese contract laborers, who were in the same degraded social position as slaves, joined the ranks of the suicides. Between 1855 and 1857, there were twice as many suicides as homicides investigated. At least one-third of the suicides were black slaves, and another one-third were Chinese contract laborers. In 1862, 346 suicides were reported: 173 Chinese, 130 black slaves, and the rest among the free colored and the whites.[41] Throughout the nineteenth century in Cuba, suicide remained popular as a quick and certain means of escape from slavery.

Growing Concern about Survival of the Slave Population

As long as the African slave trade continued unchallenged and the dead could be replaced at a reasonable price, the high mortality rate did not preoccupy the colonial authorities. Male labor was preferred on the sugar estates, and many more male slaves were brought to the sugar colonies

[40] A.H.N. Ultramar, Legajo 3550, Expediente 17, No. 10, Consulta del Consejo de Ministros, August 20, 1852.

[41] Fernando Ortiz, *La hampa afro-cubana: Los negro esclavos* (Havana: Ruiz y Cª, 1916), p. 392.

23

than female. Natural reproduction of the slave population was not encouraged in sugar colonies; it was held to be cheaper to buy than to breed, since a child was an expense for its first twelve years of life.[42] Masters considered pregnancies among their slaves to be a costly nuisance.

Sources from St. Domingue indicate masters calculated that the work of a *negresse* during an eighteen-month period (that is, the last three months of pregnancy and the months during which she breast-fed her infant) was worth 600 livres, and that during this time she was able to do only half of her normal work. The master therefore lost 300 livres. A fifteen-month-old slave was not worth this sum.[43] On the Sucrerie Cottineau, where the work force of 150 slaves had to be completely renewed between 1765 and 1778, the only question was that of purchases. To keep up the work force, the conservation and increase of children born on the estate were never mentioned by any of the managers nor by any of the absentee owners. They counted only upon acquisitions, and hoped that the coffee market would collapse, providing a healthy buyers' market for choice slaves.[44] Until the African slave trade was seriously challenged, British planters in Jamaica were hostile toward the occurrence of pregnancies among their slaves.[45] During the early nineteenth century, Francisco d'Arango y Parreño, the father of the slave plantation system in Cuba, defended Cuban planters against the charge of forced breeding in the following terms. During and after pregnancy the slave is useless for several months, and her nourishment should be more abundant and better chosen. This loss of work and added expense comes out of the master's pocket. It is he who pays for the often ineffective and always lengthy care of the newborn. This expense is so considerable that the Negro born on the plantation "costs more when he is in condition to work than another of the same age bought at the public market would have cost."[46] In the sugar colonies, then, there was almost exclusive reliance upon the African slave trade to maintain the

---

[42] Deerr, *History of Sugar*, vol. 2, p. 277.

[43] Hilliard d'Auberteuil, *Considerations sur l'état*, vol. 2, p. 65.

[44] Debien, *Plantations et esclaves*, pp. 50, 51.

[45] Patterson, *Sociology of Slavery*, p. 105.

[46] *Recueil de diverses pièces*, Requête rédigée par l'alferez-major de la ville de la Havanne, M. Francisco d'Arango et Parreño, par commission du corpe municipal, du Consulat et de la Société patriotique et addressée aux Cortès par ses corporations, p. 54.

slave labor force, and little concern about reducing the high mortality and low reproduction rates.

As the continuation of the African slave trade came increasingly into question, however, reduction of the mortality rate and encouragement of natural reproduction among the slaves became a major preoccupation of the colonizing powers. These concerns are evident in all the sugar colonies. Hilliard d'Auberteuil called for greater care to preserve the lives of the slaves because

it is certain that the slave trade cannot maintain itself much longer. The further it penetrates into the interior of Guinea, the more expensive the slaves become. We must therefore encourage the population of the blacks, and forbid masters, under severe penalties, to maintain on their plantations a destructive economy. . . . It is not sickness which weakens the population of the blacks. It is the tyranny of the masters. It has triumphed over the efforts of nature.[47]

A Spanish slave code dating from 1785 stated that it was urgent to foment procreation and marriage among slaves in order to compensate for the scarcity that was noted on the coasts of Guinea.[48] While Jamaica had been annually losing 7,000 slaves, or 2.5 percent of its slave population, with the end of the African slave trade, diminution of the slave population was scarcely perceptible.[49] Santa Lucia and Granada increased the importation of female slaves before the end of the slave trade.[50] Reform efforts in the British West Indies were successful, and the end of the African slave trade did alter the sexual imbalance and reduce the mortality rate among slaves in the British West Indies.[51]

In contrast, reform efforts failed in Cuba. The African slave trade, now outlawed by international treaty, continued to be the cornerstone of the slave system in nineteenth-century Cuba, where the sexual imbalance continued to be particularly severe. Correction of the sexual imbalance on Cuban sugar estates was often discussed, but little was accomplished.[52]

[47] Hilliard d'Auberteuil, *Considerations sur l'état*, vol. 2, pp. 62, 63.
[48] C.N.C., Cap. 26 and 146. Reform laws formulated during this period are dealt with in the section "The Bourbon Reform Period," in Chapter 5 below,
[49] Humboldt, *Island of Cuba*, p. 229 n; Patterson, *Sociology of Slavery*, p. 98.
[50] Humboldt, *Island of Cuba*, p. 229.
[51] *Ibid.*, p. 229 n; Patterson, *Sociology of Slavery*, p. 98.
[52] Arthur F. Corwin, *Spain and the Abolition of Slavery in Cuba, 1817–1886* (Austin and London: University of Texas Press, 1967), p. 111.

The Cuban system was to exclude female slaves from the sugar estates, and during the early nineteenth century very few women were present. Women slaves were sold for one-third less than men in Cuba, while in the British colonies, the price was the same for both sexes. There was a moral justification for this policy. Francisco d'Arango y Parreño explained that "until recent times, the moralists sharply disapproved the presence of both sexes on our country estates without marriage, although they found nothing criminal in condemning to eternal celibacy those who were born and had lived in absolute polygamy." [53] To correct the sexual imbalance, he proposed a special tax on estates with few female slaves. The reaction of the Cuban planters was extremely hostile. [54] Baron von Humboldt suggested the following means to relieve the decline in the slave population on Cuban estates:

1. Increase the number of female slaves
2. Relieve them from hard work during pregnancy
3. Give greater care to slave children
4. Establish slave families in separate cabins
5. Provide abundant food
6. Increase the number of days of rest
7. Allow the slaves a system of moderate labor on their own account [55]

During the early nineteenth century, some efforts were made by the Spanish authorities to encourage the presence of female slaves on the estates. They continued to allow free traffic in African slaves for twelve more years for Spanish slave traders and for six more years for foreign slave traders. The governor was instructed to see that women slaves were placed on the estates until those desiring marriage were married, "letting the owners know that aside from thus accomplishing a duty of justice and conscience, there would result for them the benefit of increasing the number of their slaves and improving their species, without the constant disbursement of their capital in buying *bozal* Negroes to replace those who die." [56]

---

[53] *Receuil de diverses pièces*, pp. 56, 57.
[54] Baron de Humboldt, *Ensayo político sobre la isla de Cuba* (Havana: Publicación del Archivo Nacional de Cuba, 1960), p. 291.
[55] Humboldt, *Island of Cuba*, p. 229.
[56] *Receuil de diverses pièces*, Real Orden, April 22, 1804, p. 58.

If the Spanish authorities expected to correct the sexual imbalance so that a creole slave population could be produced before the legal end of the African slave trade, they were certainly disappointed. The census of 1817 showed 60,322 female and 106,521 male slaves. In 1771, the ratio of female to male slaves was 1 to 1.9. By 1817, the ratio had altered slightly, 1 to 1.7. In the rural areas, the disproportion was much sharper. In 1818 in the District of Batabanó, which had 13 sugar and 7 coffee estates, there were 2,226 male and 257 female slaves, a proportion of 8 to 1. In the District of Felipinas, there were 2,494 male and 997 female slaves, or 2.4 to 1. On all the sugar estates, the proportion was barely 4 to 1.[57]

The situation had not markedly improved by the late 1840s, when intensification of international pressures to end the slave trade and slave uprisings in Cuba frightened Cuban planters into demanding the end of the illegal African slave trade. Under these circumstances, the problem of survival of the work force was sharply posed. Captain-General O'Donnell predicted economic ruin if the slave trade actually came to an end.

. . . the propagation of the creole Negro race does not fill the vacuum caused by sickness and death, because the proportion between births and death among the colored people is one to five, and propagation cannot increase, because the number of females is very inferior to that of males, as we have just seen in the departments of the Center and the West, where among a slave planation work force of 400 to 700 Negroes, not a single female exists.[58]

The Captain-General was ordered to keep a strict, secret census of the slave population, to encourage marriage among slaves, and to try to raise the rate of reproduction from 1 percent to 2 percent annually. Female slaves working in domestic service were to be forced onto plantations by the placement of a higher capitation tax on domestic slaves; a higher capitation tax was also placed on plantations with less than 10 percent female slaves.[59] By 1855, in the Cuban rural areas, there were 147,725

[57] Humboldt, *Island of Cuba*, pp. 215–16.
[58] A.H.N. Ultramar, Legajo 4655, Expediente 181, Raza Blanca y de Color, Carta de O'Donnel al Sec. de Estado, February 15, 1845.
[59] *Ibid.*

male and 79,731 female slaves between 12 and 60 years of age, and 65,350 slave children under 12.[60] By 1865, there was still a complaint from the Ayuntamiento de Matanzas that there were several sugar estates without a single woman present.[61] Sexual imbalance was not the only cause for low reproduction, because even on Cuban estates where the sexes were well balanced, there was often no increase.[62] In Jamaica before the reform period, where the sexual imbalance on the estates was less severe, the birth and survival rate of slave infants was very low.[63] However, reform efforts succeeded in the British West Indies and failed in Cuba where the slave population continued to be consumed rapidly until well past the mid-nineteenth century, and depended upon the African slave trade for survival.

Was this constant consumption of the slave population in nineteenth-century Cuba inevitable? It is true that Cuban sugar was taking over the world market and that the industry was vital and flourishing, while the industry in the British West Indies was declining. The instability and competitiveness of the sugar market encouraged a rapid using up of the slave population through overwork. The semi-mechanized condition of the sugar estates further aggravated working conditions. Nevertheless, there were reports of some well-managed sugar estates in nineteenth-century Cuba where the slave population reproduced itself naturally, without constantly resorting to the African slave trade to replenish the labor supply. Two sugar estates that belonged to a highly intelligent Havana merchant were noted for the great number of children born on them. On some coffee estates, however, where the slaves were deprived of sufficient rest, there was a low birth rate.[64]

INSTITUTIONALIZATION OF THE ILLEGAL AFRICAN SLAVE TRADE

The African slave trade, stimulated and partially organized by Cuban sugar planters, began as a subsidiary business of the sugar industry. As the

---

[60] Ortiz, *Los negros esclavos*, p. 306.

[61] Moreno Fraginals, *El ingenio*, p. 156. On the other hand, Dr. Franklin W. Knight wrote, "My own research did not reveal a general tendency towards extreme sexual imbalance by the middle years of the nineteenth century. It was in the region of 2 : 1.5." Franklin W. Knight to Gwendolyn Midlo Hall, September 13, 1970.

[62] Wurdemann, *Notes on Cuba*, pp. 153–54.

[63] Patterson, *Sociology of Slavery*, pp. 94–113.

[64] Wurdemann, *Notes on Cuba*, pp. 153–54.

demand for slaves increased, the slave trade was taken over by Spanish commercial interests that had more capital. After 1819, when the African slave trade became illegal, the importation of contraband slaves became one of the most profitable businesses in the world and realized 200 to 300 percent profit on invested capital. The illegal traffic supplied the Cuban planters abundantly with relatively cheap slaves, at least until 1830. The number of slaves introduced increased annually. Spanish commercial interests consolidated their control over the Cuban sugar industry and emerged as the principal economic beneficiary. Operating with ample capital, the commercial interests not only survived but benefited from the instability of the sugar market.[65]

It seems likely that commercial interests relying on the African slave trade were a factor undermining reform efforts. Noel Deerr concluded that "maintenance of the level of the population by natural means would not have met with the approval of the shipping and trading interests."[66] But in nineteenth-century Cuba, another powerful interest was added to the shipping and trading interests. While collecting bribes for each slave illegally brought to Cuba, parasitic government officials in both Cuba and Spain vehemently defended the illegal slave trade as an absolute necessity for the island's continued prosperity. In this respect, Captain-General O'Donnell did not differ from the typical official; during the first year of his administration, he was known to be more of an accomplice than an opponent of the slave trade.[67] But Cuban planters became increasingly dissatisfied with the African slave trade, for the prices of slaves were rising, there was a shortage of supplies, and the internal stability was being threatened by large numbers of recently arrived Africans on the estates. Following the suppression of the Conspiracy of the Ladder, many influential Cuban planters, hoping to undermine the stranglehold that Spanish commercial interests had on the Cuban sugar industry, called for an end to the African slave trade. A report of the *Sociedad Económica de Amigos del País* expressed its opposition to the continuation of the slave trade, even though agriculture would suffer from lack of labor; in addition, the report went so far as to hint that independence-minded creoles could utilize slaves

[65] Moreno Fraginals, *El ingenio*, pp. 143–44.
[66] Deerr, *History of Sugar*, vol. 2, p. 277.
[67] Corwin, *Spain and Abolition*, pp. 80, 81.

for military purposes.[68] Captain-General O'Donnell was vehemently opposed to ending the slave trade. A penal law against the African slave trade was enacted in 1845.[69] O'Donnell published the law in the *Diario de la Habana*, and sent a copy of the newspaper to Madrid with the following comment:

At the same time, I have disposed that it should not be reprinted in any other newspaper of the Island, to avoid its being diffused too much among the towns and in the countryside, which would have dangerous consequences to the tranquility and security of this territory, especially among the masses of colored people, free and slave, because, although this law has no direct relationship to the present situation of the various classes of the black race already present in the country, it could be misinterpreted, or rather exploited by the enemies of the peace and prosperity of this Island, and be the origin of turbulences.[70]

The metropolis, under intense pressure from Britain, began to explore seriously the means of ending the African slave trade. Captain-General O'Donnell's bitterness is evident in his official correspondence. Pointing out that the African population, upon which the rude tasks of the countryside weighed in that essentially agricultural country, had already diminished considerably with the absolute prohibition of the African slave trade, he gloated: "It has been the very proprietors of the big estates who, in their time, provoked and supported this measure. Perhaps they believed that tolerance would continue, and that the law would be evaded. The result should demonstrate that even against my convictions, I fulfill and see that others fulfill faithfully the orders of Your Majesty. . . ."[71]

By the end of the 1840s, 38,000 Cuban slaves had been transferred from abandoned *cafetales* to sugar estates,[72] and an estimated 30,000 Chinese laborers had entered through the port of Havana between 1847 and 1853, but the African slave trade continued. According to reports,

[68] A.H.N. Ultramar, Legajo 3557, Expediente 26, Informe de la Sociedad Económica de Amigos del País de la Isla de Cuba, May 20, 1844.
[69] For provisions of this law, see Corwin, *Spain and Abolition*, pp. 85, 86.
[70] A.H.N. Ultramar, Legajo 3550, No. 308, Carta de O'Donnell al Sec. de Estado, April 26, 1845.
[71] A.H.N. Ultramar, Testimonios . . . para averiguar . . . suicidio de los esclavos, Carta de O'Donnell al Sec. de Estado, September 18, 1847.
[72] "Report of Her Majesty's Commissary Judge at Havana," dated January 1, 1849, in Madden, *Island of Cuba*, Appendix, p. 194.

it had been reorganized under the Duchess of Rianzares, mother of Isabel II, and merchants and officials, like Antonio Parejo, Manuel Pastor, and José Forcade, were importing thousands of African slaves on the claim that they came from Brazil.[73]

It is clear that corrupt officials as well as Spanish commercial interests profited by the constant depletion of the slave population. It would not be farfetched to conclude that efforts at reforming the slave regime and ending the African slave trade in nineteenth-century Cuba foundered because those in control of state power did not find such reforms consonant with their own pecuniary interests.

[73] Corwin, *Spain and Abolition*, pp. 111, 112. For conditions among Chinese contract laborers in Cuba, see Deerr, *History of Sugar*, vol. 2, pp. 403, 404; and Moreno Fraginals, *El ingenio*, p. 154.

III

MAGIC, WITCHCRAFT, AND RELIGION

THE MYTH THAT THE AFRICANS accepted slavery passively is so old and well established that most historical writing on the subject has been and is seriously distorted. This distortion can be seen in the treatment of religious conversion and indoctrination. Many historians still view the slaves as passive and consider the policy of religious indoctrination abstractly; to them, it involves only the racial attitudes of the various European colonizing powers. The Iberian powers, they claim, were more liberal in their attitudes toward race and therefore eager to share the benefits of Christianity with their slaves. The Catholic Church, unlike the Protestant Churches, the argument goes, believed that all men were brothers, and it was therefore concerned that the slaves embrace the Faith. The impact of these factors upon the slave systems is stressed, and it is maintained that masters and slaves belonged to the same religion and were united into families, "if not by law, at least by religion."[1] Once we divest ourselves of the delusion that the slaves accepted their status passively, we can treat the religious question more intelligently, since policies toward conversion and indoctrination were intimately linked with the problem of controlling the slaves.

[1] João Ribeiro cited in Stanley M. Elkins, *Slavery: A Problem in American Institutional and Intellectual Life* (Chicago: University of Chicago Press, 1959), p. 78 n.

32

Most sources so universally and unequivocably describe the slaves as rebellious in attitude, word, and deed that it is hard to believe that folklore about the passive slave could have triumphed so long over the historical data. French missionaries to the West Indies, who knew the slaves well, described them as "vain and glorious,"[2] as "proud, arrogant, and majestic," and explained that all the European nations established in the Americas were obliged to treat them haughtily, never to forgive their faults, and never to show that they feared them; otherwise they would become "insolent, and more audacious in forming gangs to free themselves from their captivity."[3] If they were not punished for every fault and made examples of, they would be imitated by other slaves, and it would be impossible to control them. "If the master and Commander who have charge of their conduct do not make themselves feared, they are despised, the slaves debauch themselves, and do not work."[4] The slaves had a very high opinion of themselves, "as good as or better than of the masters they serve."[5] The blacks loved each other and willingly helped each other.[6] They attributed all vices to the whites and claimed that their bad example ruined the blacks. Referring to a black who acted immorally, they would say with disgust, "He is a miserable character who swears like a white, gets drunk like a white, steals like a white. . . ."[7] The extremely varied, sustained, and ingenious forms of resistance to slavery that were devised and practiced by the Africans are dealt with elsewhere.[8] This chapter focuses upon the Africans' response to slavery rooted in their religious beliefs, and the efforts of the colonizers to undermine these beliefs in order to control the slaves.

Fundamental religious beliefs largely determine how one perceives the world, and religious conversion is the ultimate device of social control. The African perception of man and of his relationship to the world and to his fellow man is very distinct from Western perception. Beliefs which

[2] Père Jean-Baptiste Labat, *Nouveau voyage aux isles de l'Amèrique*, 2 vols. (Paris: Editions Duchartre, 1931), 2:57–58.

[3] Jean-Baptiste Dutertre, *Histoire générale des antilles habitées par les français*, 4 vols. (Paris, 1667–71), 2:497.

[4] *Ibid.*, p. 529.

[5] *Ibid.*, p. 497.

[6] Labat, *Nouveau voyage*, vol. 2, p. 54.

[7] *Ibid.*, p. 60.

[8] See Chapter 4 below.

the European called pagan, especially the belief in magic, constituted an authority system over which the Europeans had little control. It was therefore in their interests, whenever possible, to convert the slaves to a degraded form of Christianity offering everlasting rewards in the hereafter in return for submission to slavery on earth. We shall see, however, that as St. Domingue and Cuba developed into flourishing slave plantation societies, the concern with religious conversion and indoctrination had to be sacrificed to more urgent and openly repressive means of maintaining order and stability.

Most important in our discussion of African religious beliefs is the belief in "hidden, mysterious, supersensible, pervading energy, powers, potencies, forces." The term for this power in common use in West Africa is *nyama*. Individuals are endowed with greater or lesser abilities to manipulate this power, and this ability can be enhanced through experience, education, and training. The power can be used for constructive or destructive purposes.[9] The African lives immersed in the world of spirit. It is his everyday, commonplace world—not an abstraction, but part of his immediate experience.[10] Africans recognize malevolence, especially among close associates, as a moral offense resulting in positive injury to the person who is its object, even if no overt act is committed. The Azande, for example, say that "hatred, envy, backbiting, slander, and so forth go ahead and witchcraft follows after."[11] The Ewe of Dahomey and Togoland, and the Tiv of Central Nigeria believe that witchcraft chiefly affects the witch's own relatives.[12] Witches are not scapegoat-like personifiers of evil; they are respected members of the community, who, as long as they keep their malevolence in check, or their witchcraft "cool," create no problems. Even when their witchcraft is active and they are accused (within the framework of carefully defined procedures to prevent private vengeance) of injuring someone, they are then expected to sincerely repent and purge

[9] Geoffrey Parrinder, *African Traditional Religion* (London: Hutchinson's University Library, 1954), pp. 21–28.

[10] Michael Gelfand, *The African Witch* (Edinburgh and London: E. and S. Livingstone, Ltd., 1967), pp. 11–16.

[11] E. E. Evans-Pritchard, *Witchcraft, Oracles and Magic among the Azande* (London: Oxford University Press, 1937), p. 107.

[12] Geoffrey Parrinder, *Witchcraft: European and African* (New York: Barnes and Nobles, 1963), pp. 134, 136.

themselves of their malevolence toward the injured party. The struggle against witchcraft is a struggle against malevolence and is therefore a major mechanism for moral control in African society.[13] Even in Haiti, where Vodun has deteriorated into an exploitative mechanism, the low murder rate that existed in the countryside, at least until the late 1950s, has been attributed to widespread belief in magic.[14] African religious concepts, including the belief in magic, do not appear to contradict some of the latest theories of family dynamics as a factor in mental illness developed by existentialist psychiatry.[15]

Africans use their sophisticated understanding of the harmfulness of repression to maintain social stability. Institutionalized release constitutes an outstanding characteristic of African cultures in the Americas as well as in Africa. To revile those in power or about to assume power is not only permitted but urged. This is done consciously, so that the soul of the ruler will not be sickened by the evil thoughts held against him by those whom he may have angered. *Fiofio*, an insect, is believed to enter the body when a quarrel between intimates has not been followed by sincere reconciliation and some gesture of affection occurs at a later date between the participants to the quarrel. When hypocrisy, conscious or unconscious, is practiced, the souls of those concerned are resentful, and their owners sicken and die. The cure is to bring the quarrel out into the open so that sincere forgiveness can take place.[16] Institutionalized release was used to maintain the slave systems in the Americas. There are numerous examples in historical literature. Dutertre describes the Africans as "satirists who reveal even the slightest faults of our Frenchmen, and they cannot see them do the least reprehensible thing without making it the subject of amusement among themselves. In their work songs, they repeat all that their masters or overseers have done to them, good or bad."[17]

[13] Monica Wilson, *Good Company: A Study of Nyakyusa Age Villages* (Boston: Beacon Press, 1963), pp. 136–57.

[14] Rémy Bastien, *Religion and Politics in Haiti* (Washington, D.C.: Institute for Cross-Cultural Research, 1966), p. 47.

[15] R. D. Laing, *The Politics of the Family* (Toronto: C.B.C. Publications, 1969).

[16] Melville J. Herskovits, "Freudian Mechanisms in Negro Psychology," in Melville J. Herskovits, *The New World Negro: Selected Papers in Afroamerican Studies*, ed. Frances S. Herskovits (Bloomington: Indiana University Press, 1966), pp. 135–45.

[17] Dutertre, *Histoire des antilles*, vol. 2, p. 497.

Père Labat noted the same characteristic. "They are satirical to excess, and few people apply themselves with greater success to knowing the defects of people, and above all of the whites, to mock them among themselves. . . ."[18]

African religious concepts leave no room for fatalism, for "neither gods nor men are pawns in an all-ordering system. Where individuals are endowed with supernatural powers they derive these from spiritual helpers who respond when they are called on, but the individual is not moved like a marionette by these powers." Dahomean creation myths stress astuteness in the face of great power, maintaining a sense of humor, judging by essence rather than appearance, realism in all relationships, discretion in speech, resiliency in social situations, and taking steps to meet problems foreseen.[19]

Faith in the spiritual powers of gifted individuals does not conflict with a rational understanding of the chain of causality and the efforts of ordinary men to control their fate by non-spiritual means. The African does not believe that witchcraft is the sole cause of events. Evans-Pritchard clearly demonstrated the place that witchcraft occupies in interpretations of events when he cited the Azande's explanation for the collapse of an old granary. The Azande knew that termites ate the supports and that even the hardest woods decayed. The collapse of the granary was normal. Mystical causation entered when certain people happened to be under the granary when it collapsed and were injured. Why were they there when it collapsed? To escape the heat and sun. But why did these two chains of causality coincide in time and space? Our answer is bad luck. Their answer is witchcraft. At no point is the African willing to abandon the concept that he can, through some means, mystical or not, control his fate.[20] Legba, a Dahomean god who still figures prominently in Vodun in Haiti, personifies the free will implicit in African religion. Legba is the means of communication between man and God, since only he speaks all languages. He invented the magic charm. He is the "arch individualist who loves mischief, knows no inhibitions, recognizes no taboos, dares to challenge injustices,

[18] Labat, *Nouveau voyage*, vol. 2, pp. 57, 58.
[19] Melville J. and Frances S. Herskovits, *Dahomean Narrative: A Cross-Cultural Analysis* (Evanston: Northwestern University Press, 1958), p. 74.
[20] Evans-Pritchard, *Witchcraft, Oracles and Magic*, pp. 69–70.

even on the part of the Creator, and to expose them. . . . In the broader world-view of the Dahomeans, he is the personification of philosophical accident; of the 'way out' in a world ruled by destiny." [21]

Religion, or, in societies that define themselves in more secular terms, philosophy, determines which perceptions society validates as real. Since man can act only upon the basis of his perception of reality, the religion or philosophy of his society sharply limits his actions. It is clear that African religious concepts tended to make the slaves rebellious. The belief in magic was especially difficult to cope with. Leaders gifted with "the power" led various forms of rebellion and often inspired more respect and fear from their fellow slaves than did their masters or the colonial authorities.

Unfortunately, Western investigators do not seriously consider the possibility that belief in magic might be based upon an aspect of interpersonal relations which has been screened out of the perceptions of the modern Western mind. "Witchcraft is an imaginary offense because it is impossible," wrote Evans-Pritchard. "Since witchcraft is impossible, the fear of witchcraft and activities to counter witchcraft must be symbolic," said Dr. Field. Africans say that the white man is incapable of understanding, for he has not "the right sort of eyes." [22] Unless we embrace a crude developmentalist approach, the universality of man's belief in magic should inspire scholars to take these beliefs more seriously. Perception is severely limited by socialization,[23] and a profound alteration in the perceptions of a significant number of people in a given society brings about real innovation in a social system.[24]

EUROPEAN BELIEF IN WITCHCRAFT

When one is dealing with the historical past involving contact between very distinct cultures, it is a mistake to define Western perception as reality and non-Western perception as unreality. In addition, one must not project the post-enlightenment European mind into the pre-enlightenment past.

[21] Herskovits, *Dahomean Narrative*, p. 36.
[22] Parrinder, *Witchcraft*, p. 204.
[23] Laing, *Politics of Family*.
[24] Anthony F. C. Wallace, "Revitalization Movements," *American Anthropologist* 58, no. 2 (April, 1956):164–81.

Until the late eighteenth century, belief in magic focused upon witchcraft as a cult of evil was strong among the Europeans, and these beliefs had a strong impact upon their responses to their African slaves.

In 1484, Pope Innocent VIII promulgated his bull *Summis Desiderantes*, a declaration of war by the Church against witches. It has been estimated that after the promulgation of this bull, as many as 300,000 "witches" were killed in Germany alone, of whom 100,000 were killed during the seventeenth century. A single bishop in Bamberg is said to have burned 600 witches. A carefully researched study of executions for witchcraft in England records about 1,000 witchcraft burnings between 1542 and 1736. Spain had the best record for resistance against the witch-burning craze. The Inquisition protected those accused of witchcraft by taking over their trials from the secular authorities. Informed theologians and enlightened officials of the Spanish Inquisition raised doubts about the reality of the crimes confessed to, and concluded that, in any case, confession alone was not enough proof. The Inquisitor Salazar Frías examined 1,800 cases in 1611, and concluded that many accused witches were deluded and that many confessions had been extracted under torture. He maintained that "evidence of accomplices, without external proof from other parties, is insufficient to justify even arrest. . . ." He opposed further edicts and arrests and concluded that "there were neither witches nor bewitched until they were talked and written about." [25] The witch-burning craze was strong in France, where belief in witchcraft permeated the highest ranks of officialdom.

It is evident that European witchcraft beliefs influenced the type of punishments inflicted upon slaves accused of crimes in St. Domingue. Slaves were often sentenced by the authorities to be burned alive for various crimes. Aside from these official executions, slaves were often burned alive or were killed by breaking their bones with clubs or hammers under the private authority of their French masters, who were convinced that their slaves were sorcerers.[26] There were also official accusations. Colas Jambes Coupées was accused of sorcery and magic because he escaped several times from irons and prisons and because he poisoned several

---

[25] Parrinder, *Witchcraft*, pp. 17–36.

[26] *Loix*, Lettre du Ministre à M. M. de la Rochalard et Duclos, September 30, 1727.

blacks. He was also accused of running away to the Spanish part of the island, seducing and carrying off other slaves, leading an armed band which robbed passersby in broad daylight and even attacked whites, and carrying on a secret correspondence to abolish the colonies. Since the smallest details of all his crimes and activities were known by everyone in the area, it was recommended that he be promptly tortured and executed, before he escaped again.[27]

Père Labat was converted to belief in African magic during his sojourn in the Antilles. He gave several examples of clairvoyance, prophecy, and rain making by gifted Africans.[28] It is difficult, at times, to distinguish between European and African magical beliefs in Père Labat's concepts. He explained that Africans rarely committed suicide after baptism. Before baptism, they were obsessed by the devil, who appeared in various forms, incited them to hang or drown themselves, and abused them until they became so horrified by these frequent apparitions that they fell into convulsions, as if they were epileptics, gave up food and drink, and either died of natural causes or killed themselves. He explained that the world was filled, at that time, with "strong spirits," but baptism was an infallible remedy. Children were baptized at once. Adults, while receiving religious instruction in preparation for baptism, had the "ordinary exorcisms" performed on them and a cross was hung around their necks, after which the obsessions immediately ceased. He cautioned against baptizing Africans without discovering if they were sorcerers in their native land, so that baptism could be deferred until

a long experience assures that they have completely abandoned the practices they had with the devil. We know that their sorceries and malices are less to be feared when they are pagans than when they are Christians. I leave to the reader to search the reason for this fact. All I can say is that it is always true.[29]

It is clear that Père Labat was attempting to deal with the African authority system on its own terms. Government officials attempted to deal with it through repressive laws. Throughout the Americas, laws were passed outlawing assemblies of slaves for any purpose, including religious

[27] *Loix*, Arrêt du Conseil du Cap, June 4, 1723.
[28] Labat, *Nouveau voyage*, vol. 1, pp. 151–56.
[29] *Ibid.*, vol. 2, pp. 405–6.

worship. Slave priests were forbidden to practice. Laws were passed against drums, music at funerals, prayers for the dead, certain African dances, and the composition, possession, sale, or use of fetishes.[30] But while the authorities continued to attempt to stamp out African religious beliefs and practices, efforts to convert the slaves to Christianity deteriorated sharply with the growth of the slave plantation system.

Efforts to Convert the Slaves Deteriorate

The French missionary Dutertre, writing during the seventeenth century, said that there was hardly a black in all the French Antilles who was not a Christian, and who had not been "regenerated in the waters of baptism." More than 15,000 blacks had been converted, but only about 25 Indians.[31] Père Labat also indicated that the Africans were much more susceptible to Christianity than the Indians were.[32] Slaves who had been baptized in Africa without religious instruction were indoctrinated after they reached the islands. Dutertre described the blacks as "zealous Christians" who lived more Christianly than many of their masters. Black children born in the French Antilles were as well instructed as French children, "sucking up their religion with their milk."[33] Charlevoix, a missionary writing during the early eighteenth century, indicated that newly arrived slaves were given private religious instruction each day, and sent to church on Sundays and holydays. There was "zeal in these matters among our colonists," who affirmed that "the most efficacious means of ensuring their fidelity is to try to make them good Christians."[34]

As St. Domingue became more prosperous and the slave population increased sharply, attitudes toward Christianization of slaves evolved into open hostility. The Mackandal Conspiracy appears to have been the turning point. Mackandal was typical of the rebel leaders who manipulated African magical beliefs. He was a great orator, had revelations, predicted the

---

[30] Code Noir, Article 16. See also, *Loix*, Ordonnance du Gouverneur, August 1, 1704; Ordonnance des Administrateurs, January 11, 1720; C.N.C., Cap. 6 and 7, *DHFS*, vol. 3, pp. 553–72.

[31] Dutertre, *Histoire des antilles*, vol. 2, pp. 501–3.

[32] Labat, *Nouveau voyage*, vol. 2, p. 406.

[33] Dutertre, *Histoire des antilles*, vol. 2, pp. 501–3.

[34] Père Pierre-François-Xavier de Charlevoix, *Histoire de l'Isle espagnole ou St. Domingue* (Paris, 1731), pp. 501–4.

future, and convinced his followers that he was immortal. Over a period of six years, he united the maroon bands, raided the plantations, and built up a network of secret organizations on the estates. His ultimate plan was to drive all the whites from the colony. In accordance with the African belief that any means were licit to fight evil, he relied heavily upon poison to eliminate not only whites but also slaves who opposed him. He also manufactured and sold fetishes, called Mackandals, which his followers believed had magical properties. They consisted of packets containing incense, holy water, herbs, small crucifixes, and poison. On a particular day, he and his followers were going to poison the water in every house in the capital province and then make a general attack upon the whites. Mackandal was betrayed, captured, and burned alive by the authorities in 1758.[35]

The colonial authorities reacted strongly against assemblies of slaves for any purpose, including religion. Colonists were forbidden to allow the "superstitious assemblies and ceremonies which certain slaves are accustomed to hold at the death of one among them, and which they improperly call prayers."[36] In spite of protests by Jesuit missionaries, the use of Christian churches by slaves was severely restricted. The authorities claimed that "the temples of God have become the temporary refuge of fugitive slaves, and serve often as a theatre of prostitution." Churches were ordered to be closed to the slaves after sundown and between the hours of noon and 2 p.m. No slave could hold a religious office, even a minor one. To protect the security of the colony, no slave, free black, or mulatto could preach within the towns or in the countryside.[37]

By the late 1760s, concern about religious conversion and the education of slaves appeared to be confined to absentee owners living safely in France.

I cannot reflect without hurt and chagrin and without fear of the reproaches which God will have the right to make to us one day about our negligence and the state of ignorance of religion in which our slaves wallow. I am even persuaded that with a little instruction, their conduct

---

[35] C. L. R. James, *The Black Jacobins*, 2d ed. rev. (New York: Vintage Books, 1963), pp. 20–21. For the judgment against Mackandal, see *Loix*, Arrêt du Conseil du Cap, January 20, 1758. For the law declaring the sale, distribution, or purchase of fetishes or Mackandals illegal, see *Loix*, Arrêt du Conseil du Cap, January 20, 1758.

[36] *Loix*, Arrêt en Règlement du Conseil du Cap, March 11, 1758.

[37] *Loix*, Arrêt en Règlement du Conseil du Cap, February 18, 1761.

would change, and the horrible crimes which they commit would diminish in number. It is the lack of zeal on this subject on the part of the colonists which loses all. . . . I am persuaded that with more religion in the hearts of the slaves, one would arrive more easily at containing them, and that one would enjoy a great deal more tranquility on the estates.

The absentee owner even suggested that an old priest was willing to serve as chaplain on the estate. The manager refused to allow it, for he alone was responsible for the discipline and good order of the plantation and he regarded the presence of a resident ecclesiastic as very harmful. The priest would quickly become the confident, then the advocate, of the blacks, thereby sapping the authority of the manager.[38]

As the colony became more prosperous and the planters more intent upon making money and living luxuriously, little energy was spent on spiritual development.[39] The planters dominated the clergy completely. Slaveowners were pleased that their slaves lived without religious instruction. "In their opinion," said a contemporary observer, "the Catholic religion contains elements that might generate ideas of equality in the mind of the Negro."[40] Planters made intensive efforts to convert to their point of view those officials who might be in favor of religious education, as is evident in this statement made in 1767 by Governor Fénélon.

I came with all the prejudices of Europe in favor of the education which we should give in accordance with the principles of our religion. But a sane political policy as well as the strongest humanitarian considerations are against religious education. The safety of the whites demands that the blacks be kept in the most profound ignorance. I have come to believe firmly that the blacks must be managed like beasts.[41]

The quality of the clergy was nothing to boast about. Most of them were monks or priests who had broken their vows or disgraced themselves in some manner, and as punishment they were relegated to the colonies. Their

[38] Gabriel Debien, *Plantations et esclaves à St. Domingue* (Dakar: Publications de la Section d'Histoire, Université de Dakar, 1962), pp. 53, 54.

[39] James G. Leyburn, *The Haitian People* (New Haven: Yale University Press, 1941), p. 115.

[40] Girard-Chatrains, as quoted in Ralph Korngold, *Citizen Toussaint* (Boston: Little, Brown and Co., 1944), p. 39.

[41] Quoted in Gaston-Martin, *Histoire de l'esclavage dans les colonies françaises* (Paris: Presses Universitaires de France, 1948), pp. 212–13.

religious influence was limited.[42] Indeed, it was almost impossible for a conscientious cleric to function in the late colony without being accused by the planters of stirring up the slaves and undermining the foundations of the society. The Jesuits were expelled from the colony in 1764 supposedly for creating unrest among the slaves.[43] In spite of the fact that Roman Catholicism was the only recognized church in St. Domingue, the universality of its doctrines had little impact when the flourishing slave plantation society began to view religious education of slaves as a threat to its stability.

ABANDONMENT OF RELIGIOUS EDUCATION OF ESTATE SLAVES IN NINETEENTH-CENTURY CUBA

In spite of the strong clerical tradition in the Spanish colonies and the scrupulous attention paid to Christianizing the slaves in seventeenth- and eighteenth-century Cuba,[44] the emergence of a slave plantation society in nineteenth-century Cuba resulted in abandonment of religious education of plantation slaves. Although rural slaves were obliged by law to be christened and buried within the Church, this became essentially a form of taxation having little or no religious significance. Fees were charged for the burial of slaves—even of infants—and private cemeteries were rarely allowed on the estates.

The dangers of carrying Christian fervor too far were brought home by the experience of the Conde de Casa Bayona who, in 1790, in imitation of Christ, humbled himself before twelve of his slaves, washed their feet, set them at his table, and served them a meal. But the slaves, instead of behaving like the Apostles, exploited the prestige conferred on them by their master's behavior, led an uprising among their fellow slaves, and burned down the estate. The twelve slaves were hunted down and their severed heads were exposed on pikes.[45]

By the late eighteenth century, both the Church and the planters began to lose interest in maintaining chaplains on the estates. The fees collected

[42] Korngold, *Citizen Toussaint*, p. 19.
[43] Leyburn, *Haitian People*, p. 116.
[44] Herbert S. Klein, *Slavery in the Americas: A Comparative Study of Virginia and Cuba* (Chicago: University of Chicago Press, 1967), pp. 87–104.
[45] Manuel Moreno Fraginals, *El ingenio: El complejo económico social cubano del azucar* (Havana: Comisión Nacional Cubana de la UNESCO, 1964), p. 49.

by the chaplains were not being passed on to the Church. The estate owners preferred to do without the added expense of maintaining the chaplain
and paying his fees. By the 1790s, estate owners began to neglect paying
tithes to the Church. The Real Cédula of April 4, 1804, provided that
newly established sugar estates would pay no tithes and that existing estates
would continue to pay tithes based upon their production in 1804. "Thus
the new economy liquidated the most solid and visible of the old feudal
superstructures." [46]

By 1820, attention to religion on the sugar estates was formal, empty,
and perfunctory. Prayers were repeated by the slaves before they went to
work in the morning and before they returned to their dormitories after
work. These were the limits of the slaves' exposure to Christianity. [47] A
rural Cuban priest spoke during the 1830s of the "good old system of
having an *oratorio* and a chaplain on each estate," but the practice had
fallen into abeyance all over the country. In general, a field slave's church
visits were restricted to the one that he made for his baptism. If the *ingenio*
(sugar plantation) or *cafetal* (coffee plantation) was close to a town,
however, a few favored slaves were allowed to go to church when the crop
season was over. [48]

Church authorities, with some support from the Crown, tried to prevent
the Church from being totally undermined by the needs of plantation agriculture. After the insurrections of the mid-1840s, when the metropolis
was trying to insure a supply of creole slaves in Cuba and reduce the
mortality rate among rural slaves, the Church tried to regain a foothold
in the Cuban countryside by suggesting Christianization as a means to
conserve these "useful hands." (This was necessary because each year an
increasing number of slaves were rendered useless for service after they
were punished for insubordination, theft, homicide, and other crimes.)
The Sección de Ultramar stressed moralizing and indoctrinating these "unfortunate beings [*seres desgraciados*]" and recommended congregations
of clergy, both Cuban and European, who would circulate throughout the

---

[46] *Ibid.*, pp. 46–55.
[47] J. G. F. Wurdemann, *Notes on Cuba* (Boston: James Monroe and Co., 1844),
pp. 169, 258; Fernando Ortiz, *La hampa afro-cubana: Los negros esclavos* (Havana:
Ruiz y Cª, 1916), pp. 185, 199 n, 371.
[48] David Turnbull, *Travels in the West Indies* (London, 1840), p. 285.

island and "exercise in the estates the sacred mission of teaching and indoctrinating."[49]

Christianization of the slaves on the rural estates had been admittedly abandoned. A high Cuban official said: "It is not necessary to have lived very long in our countryside to know that with few, but very honorable exceptions, the slaves have hardly more religion than the stupid idolatry which they brought from their country of birth."[50] Another official spoke nostalgically of the good old days when laws requiring religious education of slaves were enforced. Many sugar estates still had the "ruins and debris of their old *oratorios*, testifying to the faith of our fathers as well as to our fall and our neglect." Then, he claimed, there were no suicides. Uprisings and conspiracies contained now by force were "completely unknown, because religious instruction is the most efficacious remedy for the inconveniences which follow from slavery."[51]

It is hard to discover humanitarian sentiments in the discussion, even from the advocates of religious education. It was presented as a splendid device for controlling the slaves, convincing them to labor diligently and peacefully, and not destroy themselves, "so that their customs improve, to the profit of the State and of their masters [*para que sus costumbres se mejoren conprovecho del Estado y de sus dueños*]."[52] Here is a typical argument favoring religious education:

Without religion to control them, they will never carry out well the tasks which are assigned to them, nor be loyal to their masters. Without religion which teaches them and directs them, containing them with the thought that beyond this world, place of trials, there is another of ineffable and eternal glory for those who here suffer with resignation their misfortunes and fulfill with exactness their duties, and of endless torment for the bad, it is materially impossible for them to serve well nor attempt to conserve a life which is for them an insupportable weight. Caught between the lash and labor which they detest, and a quick, instantaneous death, they

---

[49] A.H.N. Ultramar, Legajo 4655, Expediente 181, Raza Blanca y de Color, Informe de la Sección de Ultramar del Consejo Real, December 22, 1846.

[50] A.H.N. Ultramar, Legajo 4655, No. 816, Testimonios del expediente formado para averiguar las causes que influyen en el frecuente suicidio de los esclavos, Informe de Regino Martin, October 27, 1846.

[51] *Ibid.*, Dictamen de Fiscal Olañeta, December 6, 1845.

[52] *Ibid.*, Comunicación de la Regencia de la Audiencia de la Habana al Gobernador Civil, n.d.

frequently choose the latter, because they are either totally lacking in any concept of the Other Life or they have a mistaken one, obscured by idolatry. The consolation which our Divine Religion offers to the unfortunate makes them endure not only with resignation, but even contentment [*complacencia*] the privations and labors consequent to servitude.[53]

The bishop of Havana insisted that religious education would effectively prevent suicide among the slaves and that the secret right which the clergy had possessed to investigate masters to see that their slaves were not abused should be restored. He insisted that religious instruction could be given only by priests trained in the fundamental truths of the Faith, and he requested the establishment of a monastery of thirty Franciscans to preach among the slaves.[54]

Those officials advocating revival of religious education quickly became converted to the opposing point of view. One official expressed doubt that the missionaries would serve as examples of morality, and even more important, "it would be very difficult to reconcile the Catechism with the respect which is owed to property and the utility of avoiding meetings of numerous slaves which could endanger the security of the towns." He became sarcastic about the role of the missionaries in the Conquest who "defied all kinds of dangers and often shed prodigious amounts of blood [*que Arrostraban toda clase de peligros y heran a menudo prodigos de su sangre*]. . . ." But missionaries were not appropriate to all times, places, and circumstances. Cuba did not have them, nor did she need them. The catechizing of the slaves was not the task of the missionaries, but of the masters. Prayers were led by the person on the estate who knew them best—whether the master, the manager, or the overseer. The Código Negro Español of 1789, which provided that religious instruction should be given by ecclesiastics, was suppressed in various places in America, including Cuba, and "there is no trace of His Majesty's having insisted upon its execution and fulfillment."

The matters of the Indies have become so specialized that what is most simple in theory, most useful in appearance, tends not to be applicable . . . and to be more susceptible to causing evil and disturbances. The *Bando de*

---

[53] *Ibid.*, Dictamen de Fiscal Olañeta, December 6, 1845.

[54] *Ibid.*, Informe de Excmo. Sor. Francisco Obispo de la Habana, March 6, 1847, forwarded by the captain-general to the *Regente de la Audiencia Pretorial de la Habana*, March 16, 1847.

gobernacion y policia of 1842 provided that the *master*, not an ecclesiastic should give religious instruction to the slaves.

The fiscal went on to justify this concept.

And who can better exercise the duty of catechizing the slave than his legitimate master? The serf expects all and has all from his master. His voice reaches his heart, inspires his will, disposes of his physical force, and exercises over all his being an absolute domination. His words produce an irresistible effect, and if they arise from a truly Christian stimulus, they carry along with them the gentle incentives of a Holy Religion which provides the resources to endure the evils of servitude, converts him into a grateful and appreciative creature in the eyes of the Creator and guarantees him the enjoyment of everlasting good, regardless of the color of his skin, or of his status.

When we get past the rhetoric and reach the essential point, we see that the fiscal is bluntly stating that preaching cannot be performed in the countryside, neither on separate estates nor in places where the work force of several estates could gather for the purpose of hearing the Divine Word, because he will not allow it.

We cannot ignore the security police with which the proposed missions would be very little compatible, for obvious and well-known reasons about which it is not necessary to explain, nor to go into unpleasant details [*desender a detalles acaso odiosos*]; motives which a sad experience will quickly confirm if, against the wishes of the undersigned, the missions are established.

The fiscal propounded a trickle-down theory of religious education. "Procure the morality of the masters, and it is very sure that it will be quickly transmitted to the slaves."[55]

The intendant of Cuba endorsed the trickle-down theory, emphasizing religious education for those whites living in the countryside, and the improvement of the zeal and the morality of the priests. The proposed missionaries, he feared, would not know enough about "the kind of slaves we have, nor of the manner in which they must be governed, nor of their alimentation and habits, nor of their tendencies, nor of their ignorance, nor of the complete submission in which it is absolutely necessary to keep them." The intendant also feared that some of the missionaries might be imbued with abolitionist sentiments, and he cited the fate of missionaries

[55] *Ibid.*, Respuesta del Sr. Fiscal Olivares, April 12, 1847.

in the British Caribbean who had been insulted and nearly killed by the planters on the mere suspicion that they harbored abolitionist sentiments. This same experience recurred throughout the Caribbean, wherever missionaries came into contact with slaves, because

the abolitionist societies have already made their point when they have convinced the slave that their master is their brother, their equal, that for them and for him there is only one supreme law, the same recompense and the same punishment; as soon as the mildness . . . of the missionaries contrasts unfavorably with the imperious and strong action of the master; as soon as the one was seen by the slaves as their constant protector and the other as their inflexible Lord; as soon as the counsel of Submission and Obedience to the orders of the master becomes transformed by the primordial idea that in all matters, the exact fulfillment of the duties which religion imposes is primary.

The intendant insisted that stationing ecclesiastics to serve as chaplains to the slaves on the estates for the purpose of religious instruction was completely out of the question. "There were such, a few years ago. And if experience with the result had not persuaded us to change in time, we would have perhaps found ourselves in the same position as most of the English and French Antilles." [56] The problem presented by the priest who was stationed on the estates was that he, "isolated and without occupation, little by little tries to mix into the government of the slaves, and is placed in a hostile relationship with the whites who direct the labors and tasks of the countryside, accusing them implicitly of excessive work and punishments, and finishing by converting into hatred the respect which the slaves had for their master." The ecclesiastics in Cuba, according to the intendant, should confine themselves to giving religious instruction to whites, thereby preparing the white overseers to transmit to the slaves "the first notions of religion, industriousness, and submissiveness." The sovereign powers (*facultades dominicas*) of the masters should not be reduced, even indirectly, and the slaves should not be given the least reason to suspect that their rights might be augmented. The articles of the Real Cédula of 1789 "which created such alarm among the proprietors of the Island remain and shall remain in suspension." [57]

[56] Slavery had already been abolished in the British West Indies, and was being abolished in the French West Indies during this period.
[57] A.H.N. Ultramar Testimonios . . . para averiguar . . . suicidio de los esclavos, Informe del Conde de Villanueva, Havana, June 30, 1847.

All the colonial officials fell into line, and the Audiencia Pretorial de la Habana pronounced against religious education of slaves by ecclesiastics because "there are inconveniences of some transcendence, founded in the domestic economy, regime, danger and situation of all slave countries." The Audiencia found it inconvenient to have priests carry their Catechism onto the plantations to preach to the slaves, for it was impossible for ecclesiastical or governmental authorities to dictate reforms from which "one might fear the least inconvenience to the prejudice of the slave-owners, or which might resist to some extent just respect to their property, and considerations which their difficulties and dangers demand."[58]

The metropolis pretended to ignore the opposition of colonial officials. The queen of Spain recommended that thirty or forty ecclesiastics volunteer to instruct the slaves on the rural estates, acting under the direction of the Royal Bishop [Real Obispo]. They were to be distributed among the parishes and exercise their functions on the rural estates during rest hours and on days set aside for the purpose, with the agreement of the masters. Funds for the project were to be supplied by the Junta de Fomento (Chamber of Commerce) of Cuba, and Cuban officials who participated in the discussion should suggest other means to finance the project.[59]

By the end of the year, a new captain-general, the Conde d'Alcoy, took command. He communicated his disapproval of the proposed missions, since even the remote idea of such a project caused alarm among the proprietors. He forwarded a report of the Junta de Fomento endorsing the remarks of the intendant in opposition to the proposed missions and stating further that since it had no funds to finance the project and "since this is a purely religious matter which should greatly affect the tranquility of the Island, it is up to the Governor to provide the funds."[60]

Several years later, there was a pathetic plea from the Real Obispo de la Habana calling attention to the "growing evil of suicide among slaves in the Island of Cuba," adding that since the matter had not been resolved,

[58] Ibid., Auto de Audiencia, April 14, 1847.

[59] A.H.N. Ultramar, Legajo 4655, Raza Blanca y de Color, Informe de Navaro, Madrid, November 30, 1847, Con la nota fecha, January 1, 1848, Reina—Conforme; A.H.N. Ultramar, Legajo 4655, Suelta, Carta al Gobernador Capitan-Général de Cuba, January 10, 1848.

[60] Ibid., Abstract of Carta no. 152, del Gobernador Capitan-Général de la Isla de Cuba, remitiendo en copia el informe de la Junta de Fomento en el expediente sobre evitar los frequentes suicidios de los esclavos, October 8, 1848.

two convents for missionaries should be built, one in Havana and the other in Guanabacoa, to receive ecclesiastics from the Franciscan Order "because without this help, it is completely impossible that the secular clergy, reduced to seven parishes in a city of 200,000 souls, can carry out its mission as it should, much less in the country towns where ministers are so scarce."[61]

In response to the pleas of the *Real Obispo*, the Consejo de Ministros was inspired to pronounce a few impotent abstractions. "Our Holy Religion is eminently civilizing, softening customs, dominating the proudest and most violent character, and giving the necessary conformity to endure all kinds of labor and penalties with the hope of obtaining in the other life a reward for this very resignation." Admitting that the religious education of slaves in Cuba was "abandoned to a pitiful extreme," the Consejo consoled itself with the thought that

those who have been in the country longer do not commit suicide so easily, because they are already more civilized, because their preoccupations which they brought with them from their country are already dissipating, and because their errors are lessening under the impact of the radiant light of the *evangelio*, whose clarity has begun to penetrate into their understanding.[62]

The *potestad domínica* (sovereign power) of the master continued unchallenged.

RELIGIOUS EDUCATION AND SOCIAL STABILITY

It is evident that conversion and indoctrination of the slaves into a degraded form of Christianity, which stressed submissiveness on earth in return for rewards in the hereafter, tended to undermine the authority system based upon magical beliefs, which the Africans brought with them to America. These conversions were often more apparent than real. In Africa, the conquest of one people by another meant the mutual interchange or acceptance of the respective deities. The conquerors added to their own pantheons the gods of those whom they had conquered so that

[61] *Ibid.*, Por el Ministerio de Gracia y Justicia, se remite al estado Sec. del Despacho, una comunicación del R. Obispo de la Habana, July 31, 1851.

[62] A.H.N. Ultramar, Legajo 3550, Expediente 17, No. 10, Consulta del Consejo de Ministros, August 20, 1852.

these forces would not wreak a supernatural vengeance upon them; to the conquered, the power of the gods of those who had defeated them was self-evident.[63] There was a great deal of acceptance of the outward forms of Christianity, but the basic content of the religion remained African.[64] Even in the United States, where the slave trade was less extensive during the nineteenth century, and where enforced acculturation of the largely American-born slave population during the nineteenth century assured a more stable slave system than in Latin American countries, there remains a strong African content among independent black religious sects. It is manifested, philosophically, in the tendency to identify with the power of the universe and to harness this power, here and now, for the use of man.[65] The least socialized Afro-Americans retain an intimacy with the world of spirit, and the emphasis upon "soul" in the current movement for black identity is a reaffirmation of the most essential element of the African past.

In spite of the advantages which conversion and indoctrination offered in stabilizing the slave system, the intervention of ecclesiastics into the relationship between master and slave became increasingly difficult as the prosperity of St. Domingue and Cuba increased. Even in Cuba, with its strong clerical traditions, the Church's influence was nullified by the advent of the slave plantation system in the nineteenth century. What appears to emerge from these data is that the religious education of slaves in prosperous sugar colonies was viewed as an alarming intrusion into the affairs of the estates inconsistent with maintaining order and stability. The isolation of the plantation slave and his lack of contact with authority other than the master or the overseer was an elementary condition for maintaining the system. The advantages which religious conversion of the slaves offered in promoting stability were offset by this higher consideration essential to the maintenance of the slave system once the society became prosperous and the slaves in rural areas began to substantially outnumber the whites.

[63] Melville J. Herskovits, *Life in a Haitian Valley* (New York: Alfred A. Knopf, 1937), p. 290.

[64] For a bibliography of the extensive literature on syncretism and reinterpretation in Afro-American religion, see Herskovits, *New World Negro*, pp. 38–41.

[65] Herskovits, "Some Psychological Implications of Afroamerican Studies," in *New World Negro*, pp. 145–55.

IV

BLACK RESISTANCE AND
WHITE REPRESSION

T HE COLONIAL POWERS were obsessed with one overwhelming concern: containing and controlling the slaves. The masters lived in constant terror of their slaves. While there was, perhaps, an element of paranoid projection in this response, it was essentially a reaction to a very real threat. The slaves consistently menaced public order as well as the very existence of the colonies. Available records from St. Domingue point toward insidious, systematic forms of resistance which placed a considerable amount of real power in the hands of the slaves. Overt uprisings and conspiracies aimed at seizing power were more common in Cuba.

SLAVE REVOLTS IN THE SPANISH CARIBBEAN

Slave uprisings in the Spanish Caribbean were constant, and they date from the earliest years of colonization. In 1514, the importation of slaves into Española was outlawed because of the fear of uprisings. Charles V, pointing out the danger of having large numbers of black slaves in the colonies, ordered that their number not exceed one-fourth of the total number of whites and that the latter be well armed. There was an uprising of forty African slaves in Santo Domingo in 1522, and another uprising in Puerto Rico in 1527. Slaves coming from certain "ferocious" tribes were no longer to be imported, and only one African for every three whites was allowed. A law of 1532 prohibited the importation of blacks

from the island of Gelofe because this "arrogant, disobedient, revolutionary and incorrigible caste" had instigated uprisings which resulted in the
deaths of Christians in Puerto Rico and other islands. Slaves coming from
the Gulf of Benin and from Calabar successfully mutinied several times
on the slave ships carrying them to Cuba. Slaves in Cuba often cooperated
with pirates, corsairs, and filibusters. In 1537, a French corsair, fearful of
having his ship sunk by rebel African slaves and Indians, fled Havana. The
following year, Cuban slaves cooperating with another French corsair,
sacked Havana. The *cimarrones* (fugitive slaves) of Cuba cooperated with
the Indians in their uprisings against the Spanish, and the authorities considered the blacks a bad influence on the "tame Indians" (*indios mansos*).
In 1528, blacks from Española, known for their tendency to run away, were
no longer allowed in Cuba; fifty such slaves were also deported because
they incited the domestic slaves to revolt. When the alcalde of Santiago de
Cuba arrived, he found the African slaves in revolt, killing Spaniards and
Indians, and "so terrorizing the population that no one dared go out in
the street."

Another uprising was recorded in the early eighteenth century when
the British Admiral Hosier approached Havana with his fleet. The Africans
believed they were to be freed, and uprisings occurred on several estates
southwest of Havana.[1] As a result of this revolt, their owner, the Conde
de Casa Bayona, demolished several sugar and cattle estates and divided
the land to create a village of free Spanish settlers. The Conde, losing
70,000 pesos by the destruction of his estates, was praised by the Spanish
Crown for this patriotic act, a response which clearly indicates the priority
that defense held over plantation agriculture in early eighteenth-century
Cuba.[2] In 1713, slaves from the copper mines of Santiago de Cuba armed
themselves, rose up, and declared themselves free. Unrest and uprisings
continued among them until finally, during the late 1790s, the authorities
recognized their freedom.[3] In the late eighteenth century, the Calabar slaves
in Puerto Príncipe rose up and later plotted homicide against several

---

[1] For a further discussion of these uprisings, see Fernando Ortiz, *La hampa afro-
cubana: Los negros esclavos* (Havana: Ruiz y Cª, 1916), pp. 425–37.

[2] *DHFS*, vol. 3, p. 205.

[3] Herbert S. Klein, *Slavery in the Americas: A Comparative Study of Virginia
and Cuba* (Chicago: University of Chicago, 1967), p. 201.

whites. Other uprisings occurred in Camagüey, in Güines, and near Havana.[4]

The problem of controlling the slaves became extremely aggravated during the nineteenth century. Conspiracies and uprisings among the slave and free colored population took on greater proportions with the rise of the plantation system. Slaves were imported in vast numbers. Between 1790 and 1820, 385,000 slaves were introduced into Cuba. Between 1820 and 1853, 271,659 more were introduced; and 200,000 between 1853 and 1880.[5] During the early nineteenth century, Padre Felix Varela, Cuban deputy to the Spanish Cortes, proposed the abolition of Cuban slavery because he feared that the scenes of the Haitian Revolution would be reproduced in Cuba. The example of a successful slave revolt in neighboring St. Domingue; intense international pressures against continued Spanish rule in Cuba;[6] the concentration of hundreds of slaves on each sugar estate, of whom the vast majority were male and African-born, with many coming from the same tribes and maintaining strong elements of tribal social organization; the strong military tradition among those Africans most heavily represented in mid-nineteenth century Cuba; all these combined to create an extremely unstable slave system.

Because of international pressures against the African slave trade, Cuban planters had little choice about the tribal origin of their slaves. Since Spain maintained military control, more or less, of the coast of Calabar during the eighteenth and nineteenth centuries, slaves from this area of West Africa, called Carabalis, were heavily represented.[7] Colonists in the British West Indies, however, preferred slaves from the Gold Coast, since they regarded slaves from Calabar as fierce and rebellious.[8] It was said that the Carabalis were "quick-tempered and required to be watched."[9] The Lucumi (Yorubans) were also heavily represented in nineteenth-century Cuba. They

[4] Ortiz, Los negros esclavos, pp. 425–37.

[5] Ibid., p. 89.

[6] Mario Hernández y Sánchez-Barba, "David Turnbull y el problema de la esclavitud en Cuba," Anuario de Estudios Americanos, 14 (1957): 241–99.

[7] Ortiz, Los negros esclavos, pp. 30–48. This is a careful study of the actual tribal origins of the slaves referred to by the terms in common use in Cuba.

[8] Elizabeth Donnan, ed., Documents Illustrative of the History of the Slave Trade to America, 4 vols. (Washington, D.C.: Carnegie Institute, 1930–35), 1: 108.

[9] J. G. F. Wurdemann, Notes on Cuba (Boston: James Monroe and Co., 1844), p. 257.

came from a powerful kingdom northeast of Benin, almost on the Niger Delta. The Yoruban Kingdom was in the process of dissolution during the mid-nineteenth century, and many of the Lucumi were war captives.[10] Their prestige was high among neighboring tribes, who, disdaining their own language, learned the language of the Yorubans. The Lucumi were described as "strong and indomitable."[11]

The Mandingas and Gangas were considered "the most tractable and trustworthy."[12] The Mandingas occupied the entire coast of West Africa from Senegal to Liberia, and northward to the kingdoms of Ashanty and Dahomey. They were very intelligent and most of them arrived in Cuba with writing and other skills that made them highly valued. Many Mandingas and Gangas were brought to Cuba before 1830—before the English colony of Sierra Leone had been founded and before the British fleet had effectively blocked the slave trade from these regions of Africa.[13]

While poor communications and the natural tendency to suppress news of revolts so that other slaves would not follow the rebels' example, tended to minimize reporting, the recorded list of uprisings in nineteenth-century Cuba is impressive. The first recorded uprising took place in 1805. In March, 1809, the *gente de color* rebelled against the French refugees from St. Domingue and sacked their homes. A large-scale uprising involving sugar estates in the provinces of Puerto Príncipe, Holguín, Bayamo, Trinidad, and Havana broke out. The uprising in Havana was led by José Antonio Aponte, who tried to emulate Toussaint l'Ouverture. Overseers and other white dependents were killed, and factories were burned down. Slaves on many estates were involved, including most of those on two sugar estates near Havana. Aponte and eight of his accomplices were drawn and quartered and their corpses exposed on the Bridge of Chavez to terrorize the slaves. Another uprising took place in Matanzas in 1825, resulting in the sacking and burning of 24 estates, the killing of 15 whites and 43 blacks, and the wounding of 170 slaves. In 1826, another uprising occurred in Güira. Two uprisings took place on coffee estates in 1830, and

[10] Philip D. Curtin, *Africa Remembered: Narratives by West Africans from the Era of the Slave Trade* (Madison: University of Wisconsin Press, 1969).
[11] Ortiz, *Los negros esclavos*, pp. 30–48; Wurdemann, *Notes on Cuba*, p. 257.
[12] Wurdemann, *Notes on Cuba*, p. 257.
[13] Ortiz, *Los negros esclavos*, pp. 30–48.

a conspiracy against the whites of Guamacaro was discovered. In 1831, there was an uprising on the coffee estate Nueva Empresa, and in 1833 on the sugar estate Jimagua.

By the 1830s, slave uprisings were so frequent and the methods employed by the authorities to suppress them were so destructive that the *hacendados* soon realized that the intervention of the authorities was more costly than the rebellions themselves. In 1833, the Captain-General of Cuba ordered the *jueces pedáneos* (circuit judges) to stop invading rebellious estates with large bodies of armed men "killing animals and slaves and ruining their owners." There were uprisings on sugar and coffee estates during 1835 in Jaruco, Matanzas, Macurijes, and near Havana. Over 50 blacks, killing and wounding several whites, tried to penetrate the walled city of Havana. They were dispersed by a squadron of lancers. The leaders were shot and their heads were placed on the Bridge of Cristina. There was also an uprising on the same Bridge of Chavez where Aponte and his companions were drawn and quartered. In 1837, there was a slave rebellion in Manzanillo; and in 1840, in Cienfuegos and Trinidad. In October, 1841, slaves, constructing the palace of Aldama in Havana, revolted and were shot down. Uprisings occurred on estates in Managua and in Lagunillas in 1842. There was a conspiracy in 1843 among blacks of Haiti, various Americans living in Jamaica, and Cuban *gente de color*.

The large-scale uprisings that took place in Cuba in 1843, began with 254 slaves of the sugar estate Alcancia, followed by those of La Luisa, La Trinidad, Las Nieves, and La Aurora, those of the coffee estate Moscou, those of the cattle farm Ranchuelo, and those of the Cardenas to Jucaro railroad. The latter uprisings were successfully dispersed by a squadron of lancers. Many of the slaves were killed, and many fled to the mountains, where about forty hanged themselves.[14] By the middle of the decade, Cuba was rocked by revolts and widespread conspiracies. Around Trinidad, where twenty-seven new *ingenios* were established within a two-year period, an insurrection started on the estate of a Mr. Baker, who was reputed to be a hard master. Not a single female was present on the estate. Six hundred insurgents from his and an adjoining estate tried to seize a barracks at Trinidad and disarm the soldiers. A female slave on the adjoining

[14] *Ibid.*, pp. 425–37.

estate betrayed the plot to her master. Mr. Baker escaped with his life, but his estate was burned down. The insurgents were attacked by soldiers, about fifty of them were captured or killed, and the rest were hunted down in the woods. One white man and one soldier perished, and many slaves died.[15]

THE CONSPIRACY OF THE LADDER

An important uprising took place in November, 1843 on the Triumvirato, an *ingenio* in Matanzas. After damaging several neighboring estates, the insurgents were cut down by thirty horsemen from a regiment of the *Lanceros del Rey*. Fifty slaves were reported dead, and sixty-seven taken prisoner. The rest escaped into the woods and hanged themselves. This event was reported to Madrid as a normal occurrence in the countryside that did not alter the general tranquility of the country, since under no circumstances could the slaves resist the first armed force sent against them.[16]

But the authorities soon had to conclude that they had underestimated the danger. The following year, the Conspiracy of the Ladder, a far-reaching conspiracy among the slaves on estates and in towns and among the free colored population, who plotted to seize power in Cuba, was uncovered. The coordinated uprising was scheduled to erupt in March, 1844. Although it has been charged that the insular authorities took advantage of the situation to implicate in the conspiracy whatever elements of the population they felt to be potentially disloyal,[17] and that British agents, especially the former British Consul David Turnbull, were deeply implicated,[18] there is little doubt that the conspiracy among the estate slaves was very real and extraordinarily well organized. The organization had been slow and extensive, and had been carried out through the tribal organizations and dance groups of the plantations. Each plantation had also elected a king and queen. The conspiracy was not only the most premedi-

---

[15] Richard R. Madden, *The Island of Cuba* (London, 1853), p. 171.

[16] A.H.N. Estado, Legajo 8038, Expediente 22, No. 4, *Sublevación de 5 noviembre, ingenio Triumvirato, Matanzas*, Carta de O'Donnell al Prin. Sec. de Estado, November 8, 1843, Carta a O'Donnell, Capitan-General de Cuba, January 8, 1844.

[17] Francisco Gonzalez del Valle y Ramirez, *La conspiración de la escalera* (Havana: Imprenta El Siglo XX, 1925).

[18] Hernández, "David Turnbull."

tated but also the largest uprising in Cuba. Four thousand people were tried by a military tribunal; 98 were condemned to death, about 600 to prison, and over 400 deported.[19] Voluminous testimony, taken about the details of the organization of the conspiracy in each town and district, indicated that the British were expected to supply arms and to provide arsenic to be put in the water supply and that a British fleet was to arrive.[20] A slave named Joaquim Nigth was convicted for selling *brujerías* (magic charms) to make one invincible.[21] Another slave, a Ganga named Cristobal, was accused of using witchcraft to dominate the spirit of his mistress.[22] Several slaves on the *cafetal* Buena Esperanza were convicted in connection with the conspiracy for trying to poison their master.[23] Leaders of the conspiracy on the *ingenio* La Amistad held meetings in a cave where they manufactured fetishes to protect the wearers from all kinds of danger "so that the idiocy of their followers allowed them to win prestige among their blind and ignorant admirers."[24] On the *ingenio* Nueva Vizcaya and other estates in the District of Yumuri, the Lucumi slave Valentin was elected the *rey principal* of the district and Luciano, a Mandinga, described in the judgment as a "sagacious and influential man with a privileged mind

---

[19] Ortiz, *Los negros esclavos*, pp. 425–37. The reality of the Conspiracy of the Ladder has been called into question by scholars. This is a complicated problem. The evidence in Madrid is very sketchy, consisting of excerpts from testimony torn out of context to substantiate charges of British involvement in the conspiracy (A.H.N. Estado, Legajo 8057). Of two Cuban scholars who consulted the voluminous testimony which is preserved in Havana, Fernando Ortiz concluded unequivocably that the conspiracy was not only very real, but the best organized and premeditated of all the slave uprisings in Cuba. Francisco Gonzalez del Valle doubted charges made against a number of independence-minded white creoles and against members of the colored elite, but as far as I can determine did not doubt the reality of the conspiracy among the slaves. Indeed, there were a number of overt uprisings. While the conspiracy might have been exaggerated for the purposes of repression, it seems very unlikely that the charges were a pure fabrication. There are thousands of pages of testimony taken from Cuban slaves which might very well be a unique source which can answer many questions about slavery in the Americas.

[20] A.H.N. Estado, Legajo 8057, Testimony taken on the *cafetal* La Constancia, Jurisdiction of San Antonio de los Baños, July 18, 1844.

[21] *Fallos*, No. 23A, Ingenios del Partido de Guamacaro y Guanabana.

[22] *Fallos*, No. 17A, Ingenio La Luisa y otras fincas colindantes de los partidos de Macurijes y Cimarrones.

[23] *Fallos*, No. 11A, Cafetal Buena Esperanza de D. Pedro Domech y otras colindantes en Partido de la Guanabana.

[24] *Fallos*, No. 24A, Ingenio la Amistad y otras en Partidos de Lagunillas y Cimarrones.

among his class," was his counsellor. The black woman Petrona Chacon had been elected queen. Nineteen estates and over 6,000 slaves of this one district had been involved in the conspiracy. The authorities seized several wooden lances in the *rey principal*'s hut.[25] A pharmacist was punished for allowing a man of color to handle drugs.[26]

This conspiracy and its repression had a profound impact upon the economy as well as upon the slave population. The exportation of boxes of sugar (a box equaled 200 pounds) from Cuba was sharply reduced, as the following figures indicate:[27]

	Havana	Matanzas	Total
1844	528,778	299,189	827,967
1845	256,556	99,436	355,992
1846	505,983	289,112	795,095

The repression of the conspiracy was characterized by extreme cruelty and abandonment of judicial norms. The President of the Military Commission in Matanzas, charged with conducting these trials, issued instructions that "when it is a matter of the security of the country, and of a crime against the state, any means are legal and permitted if beforehand, there exists a moral conviction that the desired result will be produced, and the general welfare demands it." Those dying from starvation, under the lash, and by other forms of punishment outnumbered those sentenced and executed.[28] As many as a thousand lashes were inflicted on a single slave. Confessions obtained in this manner often implicated people not involved in the conspiracy. A number of whites, both creoles and foreigners, were arrested on such testimony, with the result that "confidence in the protection of the government was entirely lost. Abandoned to the caprice of the sub-commission that visited the plantations, the whole population, afraid to utter one word against their acts, in despair saw their prop-

---

[25] *Fallos*, No. 20A, Contra las dotaciones del ingenio Neuva Vizcaya y otras colindantes del partido de Yumurí.

[26] *Fallos*, No. 11A, Cafetal Buena Esperanza de D. Pedro Domech y otras colindantes en Partido de la Guanabana.

[27] Madden, *Island of Cuba*, Appendix, p. 190.

[28] Communicación del Brigadier Presidente de la Sección de la Comisión Militar, Fulgencía Salas, al Capitan de Infantería Mariano Paradas, en Matanzas, February 28, 1844; Causa de conspiración, c., leg. 53, pieza 3ª, cited in Gonzalez del Valle, *Conspiración de la esclera*, pp. 30, 31.

erty sacrificed, and were compelled to witness the most revolting scenes of cruelty." [29] Suicide also took a heavy toll. "The fear of being punished or implicated in the Conspiracy case discovered in Matanzas induced a great number of colored persons, free and slave, to commit suicide during the years 1843 and 1844, which are clearly the two in which suicide increased the most." [30] The slave population of Cuba drastically declined, as is evident from the following figures: [31]

Year	Slaves	Free Colored
1841	436,495	152,838
1846	326,759	149,226
1849	324,187	164,712
1855	366,421	179,012

Captain-General O'Donnell officially denied British charges of cruelty in the course of suppressing this conspiracy. He stated that "far from having made use of terror or afflictive means to clarify the facts, or proceeding with rigor in the imposition of penalties, each and every trial is resplendant with the spirit of leniency, of moderation and of justice which presided in them." He went on to explain that during the first days of the discovery of the conspiracy, when the entire extent of it was realized, to avoid further increasing the number of prisoners, which had already gone beyond 3,000, and to avoid depriving the masters of their slaves during the grinding season, several slaves who were not principal leaders were flogged on the estates; after receiving their punishment, they were returned to their masters. But these punishments, he claimed, were never employed during the trials with the free colored, much less with white men. The queen instructed him to "continue submitting data about the success of the trial of several English subjects accused of complicity in the last conspiracy, so that the Government of Her Majesty can answer with authentic data and information the reclamations directed by the British Minister concerning this matter." [32]

[29] Wurdemann, Notes on Cuba, Appendix, pp. 356–57.

[30] A.H.N. Ultramar, Legajo 4655, No. 816, Testimonios del expediente formado para averiguar las causes que influyen en el frecuente suicidio de los esclavos, Informe del Conde de Villanueva, Intendente de Cuba, Havana, June 30, 1847.

[31] Ortiz, Los negros esclavos, pp. 321–22.

[32] A.H.N. Estado, Legajo 8039, No. 78, Carta de O'Donnell al Sec. de Estado, contestando la Real Orden de 10 de julio, September 30, 1844; Contesta de La Reina, December 4, 1844.

The queen was probably less thrilled with the "spirit of leniency, moderation, and justice resplendent in the trials" when the 1846 census showed a decrease of 112,736 in the slave population since the 1841 census.[33] The captain-general explained the decrease in terms of the halt in the African slave trade. "Only in the slaves can one really ascertain a drop, because African Negroes have not been introduced during the past two years."[34] The captain-general claimed that the census was inaccurate and ordered a recount of the most populous *ingenios*, demanding that they furnish accurate figures.[35] It is estimated that the African slave trade increased during the first two years of O'Donnell's administration, but was effectively reduced during the last two years.[36] Neither the reduction in the African slave trade nor inaccuracies in the census, however, can account for the magnitude of this population loss, especially since subsequent censuses continued to reflect the drastic decline. There was a large, standing army of Spanish troops in Cuba, and the insular authorities resorted to massive destruction of the slave population to insure their continued rule.

It is probably true, as some historians have claimed, that the methods used by the insular authorities to crush the Conspiracy of the Ladder were the only means of holding the colony for Spain.[37] Massive intimidation of all who offered the threat of opposition or potential opposition, terrorization of the slave population, and destruction of the free colored elite gave Spain twenty years of relatively tranquil control in Cuba. Organized independence and abolitionist movements stagnated until the mid-1860s.

While confrontation was the major form of slave resistance in Cuba, flight and the organization of *palenques* (maroon colonies) were also important forms of resistance. *Cimarrones* were a serious problem to the

[33] See figures in table above.

[34] A.H.N. Ultramar, Legajo 4655, No. 861, Carta de O'Donnell al Sec. de Estado, November 28, 1847.

[35] *Cuadro estadístico de la siempre fiel Isla de Cuba, correspondiente al año de 1846, formado bajo la dirección y protección del Escmo. Sr. Gobernador y Capitan-General Don Leopoldo O'Donnell, por una Comisión de Oficiales y Empleados particulares* (Havana: Impr. del Gobierno, 1847), p. v. While modern scholars have doubted the accuracy of the 1846 census, subsequent censuses continued to reflect the sharp decline in the slave population. A final answer to this question must await demographic studies which are based upon materials in Cuba as well as in Spain.

[36] Arthur F. Corwin, *Spain and the Abolition of Slavery in Cuba, 1817–1886* (Austin and London: University of Texas Press, 1967), pp. 80, 88.

[37] Justo Zaragoza, *Las insurrecciones de Cuba*, 2 vols. (Madrid: Impr. de M. G. Hernández, 1872–73), 1:536.

authorities from the earliest days of the colony until the end of slavery. Governor Ovando complained, in 1503, that the blacks fled to the woods with the Indians and taught them insubordination and bad habits.[38] The *palenques*, fortified villages barricaded with trunks of trees, were frequently located in the mountains of Oriente and of Pinar del Rio or the Zapata Swamp. The *cimarrones* armed themselves with machetes, wooden arrows, and iron spears which they manufactured themselves. The *palenques* survived throughout the history of slavery in Cuba, and the authorities devoted considerable attention and resources to efforts to keep them under control.[39]

SYSTEMATIC RESISTANCE IN ST. DOMINGUE

Before the outbreak of the Haitian Revolution, there were few overt attempts to seize power in St. Domingue. We have already noted the Mackandal Conspiracy. There was also a conspiracy led by two blacks and one white *engagé* that involved slaves in Port-de-Paix. Its objective was to take over the town when the French army left, massacre all whites, and turn the city over to the Spanish army. The leaders had contacted the Spanish through a French-speaking Spanish mulatto known as l'Espion. The conspiracy never succeeded, however, and all the conspirators were tortured and killed.[40]

While overt conspiracies and uprisings were rare in St. Domingue compared with Cuba, more systematic, insidious, and, in the long run, more effective forms of resistance were practiced by the slaves of St. Domingue. Open confrontation gave way to guerilla warfare. This pattern was set quite early. The Dutch had brought 1,200 to 1,300 black slaves to Martinique and Guadeloupe before 1656, selling them cheap and on credit.[41] M. Houel, the administrator of the colony, having more confidence in his slaves than in the French colonists, made the mistake of arming his slaves and teaching them to use firearms. The slaves outnumbered the French, and at the end of 1656 there was an uprising led by two slaves named Pedre and Jean le Blanc. Their plan was to massacre the masters, keep

---

[38] Ortiz, *Los negros esclavos*, p. 398.
[39] *Ibid.*, p. 413.
[40] *Loix*, Jugement du Conseil de Guerre, November 11, 1691.
[41] Jean-Baptiste Dutertre, *Histoire générale des antilles habitées par les françois,* 4 vols. (Paris, 1667–71), 3:201.

their wives, and set up two Angolan kingdoms in Guadeloupe, one at Basse-Terre and the other at Capterre. But inter-tribal rivalries carried over from Africa led to disunity, and some of the conspirations failed to show up at the appointed time and place. About forty slaves armed themselves and seized several plantations. Pursued by the militia, they headed for the woods, where the militia hestitated to follow. For ten or twelve days, they pillaged the plantations and massacred the French settlers. The French militia obtained twenty Brazilian slaves to carry food and serve as guides to pursue the rebels, who, fleeing to the mountains, were ambushed en route. The two kings were quartered and several of their followers were subjected to penalties such as being broken on the wheel, hanged, flogged, and having their ears cut off.[42]

Simultaneously, mass desertions of slaves occurred in Guadeloupe. Slaves fled to the Indians, who received them well at first, but later discovered that they could be profitably sold to the Spanish. Deserters frequently returned to Guadeloupe for the relatives they had left behind and to convince others to follow them. Desertions became so massive that every house had lost slaves. On November 29, 1656, there was a rumor that all the slaves were going to leave. Many slaveowners followed the example of M. Chevrolier, who had put his slaves in irons. But in spite of draconian measures, mass desertion spread to even the most devoted slaves. Punishments only made them leave more quickly. "One was reduced to such an extremity at Martinique," wrote Dutertre, "that one dared not say a cross word to a black, nor make the slighest correction, without his fleeing to the woods. Even the *Negresses* instigated flight, and ran off with little infants seven or eight days old."[43]

Search parties sent after the slaves could not locate them. The blacks led groups of Indians, raiding the plantations in broad daylight, stealing, killing, running off slaves, and burning homes. This situation lasted two years, until the French authorities decided that the only solution was to clear out the Indians, who were giving the slaves boats in which to escape and offering them asylum. The French finally came to an agreement with the Indians that they were not to receive fugitive slaves.[44]

The fugitive slaves, called *marons*, developed techniques of guerilla

[42] *Ibid.*, vol. 1, pp. 500–502.
[43] *Ibid.*, vol. 2, p. 537.
[44] *Ibid.*, vol. 1, pp. 502–4.

warfare which closely resemble contemporary techniques. The tactics of Francisque Fabulé are a good example. He was a big, tall, powerful slave with a martial air. He declared himself the leader of three or four hundred *marons*, organized his followers into groups of twenty-five or thirty, and dispersed them around the island. They descended on isolated estates at night and stole arms and provisions, although they did not at first kill anyone. The settlers, fearing the possibilities of the situation, offered Francisque his freedom if he would return and bring in some of his followers. Francisque agreed to these terms but then reneged. Instead, he joined the Indians and blocked the roads, burned down estates, and massacred their owners. The French settlers decided to fight, but they did not get very far. Thick forests, rocks, cliffs, and mountains blocked their path. The French militia, after hunting the *marons* for a month, captured only five or six fugitives who happened to have foot trouble and could not run. "The rest, not at all wishing to fight, sought their health in flight." Four or five Frenchmen died of snakebite. Since the pursuit was proving more costly to the French than to the fugitive slaves, the militia asked to be demobilized to attend to their neglected crops, and the authorities adopted a new tactic: offering rewards for the return of fugitives—paying the reward and pardoning the fugitives. Since these tactics made inroads upon his following, five or six months later, Francisque agreed to surrender in return for his freedom. A treaty was signed which stated that the island was devastated by fugitive slaves, and since Francisque Fabulé was a leader of a large band, he would be given his freedom and a thousand pounds of tobacco, and no punishment would be inflicted upon the members of his band. He brought in six or seven of his followers, collected a reward, and was given his freedom, an official hug, and a sword to wear. Thereafter, he brought in large numbers of fugitives in return for additional rewards.[45]

Escaped slaves set up communities in St. Domingue, elected their own leaders, cultivated the soil, built houses, and constructed barricades against invaders. Some fugitives hid in the cane fields during the day, robbed passers-by on the highways at night, and went from plantation to plantation seizing cattle. They sometimes hid in the slave quarters and gathered information about what went on in the master's house so that

[45] *Ibid.*, vol. 3, pp. 201–4. For the treaty signed with Francisque Fabulé, see *Loix*, Arrêt du Conseil de la Martinique, March 2, 1665.

they could steal without being noticed.[46] Mass desertions of slaves, especially in wartime, were common. The authorities complained:

. . . they leave in bands, and desert to the foreigners with whom we are at war. Several of the colonists have had the misfortune of seeing themselves deprived of the cultivation of their lands, and reduced to seeking the help of their friends to provide for their families. And it is certain that . . . the enemy has not taken as many as those who have given themselves up voluntarily, and a great number who remain do so only for the return of some and the desertion of others from the Island.[47]

Colonists lived in fear of being suddenly ruined by the loss of all their slaves. Planters going to bed at night owing 100 or 200 slaves could not be sure of waking up the next morning with even one.[48]

Flight was greatly facilitated in St. Domingue because two-thirds of the island was in Spanish hands. The Spanish part of the island was undeveloped, thinly populated, its slave system relatively mild. The colonial rivalries between France and Spain made the authorities of the Spanish part of the island very uncooperative in returning fugitive slaves. Attempts to eliminate the Spanish part of the island as a refuge for fugitive slaves had little success. In 1728, a secret treaty was signed with the Spanish to allow a French agent to go to the City of Santo Domingo to claim all the fugitive slaves. The agent, le Sieur le Jeune, spent 23,700 livres in this undertaking, which was fruitless because a revolt took place at Santo Domingo when he arrived. Attempts to tax the colonists to pay for the expenses of this undertaking failed, and the cost was eventually assumed by the king of France.[49] It was not until 1776 that a treaty was negotiated between France and Spain for the purpose of mutual restoration of escaped slaves.[50]

[46] *Loix*, Arrêt du Conseil de la Martinique, October 13, 1671; Arrêt de Règlement du Conseil de Léogane, March 16, 1705.

[47] *Loix*, Arrêt du Conseil de Léogane, July 1, 1709.

[48] *Loix*, Mémoire des Administrateurs au Conseil Supérieur du Cap, July 7, 1721.

[49] *Loix*, Arrêt du Conseil du Petit-Goave, March 6, 1728; Arrêt du Conseil du Cap, December 6, 1728; Extrait de la Lettre du Ministre à M. Duclos, January 18, 1735.

[50] *Loix*, Commission d'un commissaire de la Nation françoise auprès du Gouvernement Espagnole de Santo Domingo, January 15, 1776; Ordonnance des Administrateurs concernant les Nègres Espagnoles pris en marronage, March 30, 1776; Ordonnance des Administrateurs concernant les frais de restitution des Esclaves fugitifs ramenés de l'Espagnole, April 16, 1776; Traité définitif de Police entre les Cours de France et de l'Espagne sur divers points concernant leurs Sujets respectifs à St. Domingue, June 3 and December 4, 1777; Lettre de l'Intendant à l'Ordonnateur du Cap, touchant le prix des Nègres François mariés dans la partie Espagnole, January 28, 1778.

Colonial officials were well aware of the danger implicit in the existence of these permanent pockets of slave military power. ". . . A colony which has the misfortune to have to fear establishments of slave deserters enters, from that moment, into a state of war, the danger of which can only increase with time.[51] Large maroon bands and guerilla bases were never successfully eliminated throughout the colonial period in St. Domingue, and were still in existence at the outbreak of the Haitian Revolution.[52] In St. Domingue, guerilla warfare was constant and led to eventual seizure of power. In Cuba, overt outbreaks, conspiracies, and attempts to seize power were characteristic. When abolition finally came in Cuba, it was a by-product of the Ten Years War for Cuban independence.[53]

THEFT AND THE MARKET

The market was very important to the economic, social, and religious life of West Africa, and the blacks, especially the women, were skilled in buying and selling. The French colonists depended upon the slave-operated markets to trade goods within the colony, and especially to provide the cities and towns with food. When the Code Noir of 1685 outlawed these markets, the colonial authorities protested that they were absolutely necessary to the commerce of the colony, and the French government changed the law the next year to allow them to continue.[54]

The West African brought with him complex ideas about property. In Dahomey, which had the greatest cultural influence in St. Domingue, everything belonged, in theory, to the king: land, horses, implements, slaves, money, even the person of the subject. But no king would dare to claim his rights because of fear of the ancestors. There were two other types of property. One was the property of the *sib*, or extended family. It was owned collectively and administered by the oldest male member. The other was private property, which could be held by men or women. It

---

[51] Emilien Petit, *Traité sur le gouvernement des esclaves*, 2 vols. (Paris: Knapen, 1777), 2:165. Petit was referring to a peace treaty signed between the Assembly of Jamaica and Cudjoe, leader of fugitive slaves, in 1739. A French translation of the treaty was published in *ibid.*, vol. 2, pp. 165–77.

[52] C. L. R. James, *The Black Jacobins*, 2d ed. rev. (New York: Vintage Books, 1963).

[53] Ramiro Guerra y Sánchez, *La guerra de los diez años, 1868–1878* (Havana: Cultural S.A., 1950), pp. 47–51.

[54] Code Noir, Article 7; *Loix*, Arrêt du Conseil d'Etat, October 13, 1686.

included the houses a person built and the trees he planted, regardless of who owned the land. It also consisted of the money earned, the produce of one's labor, utensils, guns, mats, pipes, and magic charms, which often consisted of herbs and medicines discovered in the forest. The discoverer could sell the formula to others for their use. There were complex rules for inheritance of personal property.[55]

French law denied all property rights to slaves. Anything the slave might acquire through industry, through gift, or in any other way, belonged legally to the master. A slave could not give or will anything he possessed to members of his family or to friends. He could not make a valid contract disposing of goods.[56] This simplistic view of property rights, entirely excluding the slave, was impossible to enforce in St. Domingue, especially since the slaves controlled the internal market, and, in addition to the legal market, an illegal one was created to dispose of stolen goods. Indeed, the illegal market tended to supplant the legal one. Colonial officials complained that slaves were stealing indigo and other merchandise that was easy to carry and selling it to black-market operators traveling from plantation to plantation; this illegal trade was thriving to such an extent that the public markets were poorly attended.[57] The *procureur du roi* described the systematic operations of the black market:

. . . several persons buy indifferently from slaves indigo, horses, clothing, and other merchandise without troubling to find out where the slaves could have obtained these goods. The slaves conspire with the house slaves to steal the indigo from the drying houses and the horses from the fields, break into the storehouses, and pass the stolen goods from one neighborhood to another, from hand to hand among the slaves until it is finally sold to several bad-intentioned individuals who receive it, give some recompense to the slaves for their thefts, and then resell it to merchants or exchange it for other merchandise.[58]

Slaves used monopoly price-fixing to profiteer on food sold in the cities and towns. Waiting along the highways, they stopped the supplies that were being sent to the market and then resold the goods at high prices.

---

[55] Melville J. Herskovits, *Dahomey, An Ancient West African Kingdom*, 2 vols. (New York: J. J. Augustin, 1928), 1: 51–63 and 78–95.

[56] Code Noir, Article 28.

[57] *Loix*, Arrêt du Conseil du Petit-Goave, January 14, 1692.

[58] *Loix*, Arrêt du Conseil du Petit-Goave, January 8, 1697.

These practices were so effective that the Conseil du Cap complained that officers from the merchant fleet, the clergy, the House of Charity, and private families were suffering from lack of eggs, poultry, and vegetables, and some people were being forced to eat meat on the days forbidden by the Church because of the lack of fresh foods.[59]

The blacks of St. Domingue used their control of the internal markets, both the legal and illegal ones, to amass sums of money so that they could purchase their freedom. Cabarets owned by free blacks became centers of vice, the proceeds of which went toward purchasing freedom for more individual slaves. The colonial officials concluded that most of the disorder among slaves came from the "facility which the colonists have of giving them freedom in return for sums of money," because once a sum was agreed upon, they

. . . abandon the service of their masters, engaging in private affairs under the pretext of working by the day in return for a small recompense which they promise to their said masters. Others abandon themselves to all kinds of vices to amass the sums agreed upon, getting together in the houses of those who have already been freed, most of them having cabarets, even among whites, who are low enough to receive them, and suffer their infamous and immodest commerce.[60]

The blacks in St. Domingue exercised a considerable amount of economic power through control of the internal market and by amassing wealth through both legal and illegal channels, much of which went toward increasing the free black population.

MURDER

If suicide was a quick and sure means of escape from slavery, murder was a means of asserting the essential equality of the slave with the master. In the black community in the United States, a weapon is called an "equalizer." The capacity to inflict death transcends the most extreme forms of social ranking. There are records of direct and unceremonious assaults by slaves upon their masters. One woman slave stabbed her master to death.[61] Another slave killed his master by hitting him on the head with

[59] *Loix*, Arrêt du Conseil du Cap, February 7, 1707.
[60] *Loix*, Ordonnance des Administrateurs Généraux des Isles, August 15, 1711.
[61] *Loix*, Arrêt du Conseil du Cap, September 9, 1779.

a hoe.[62] Generally, however, the slaves preferred more cautious and premeditated forms of murder which were less likely to be detected. The popular American folk song, "The Bluetail Fly," describes the murder of a master by a slave who pretended the master met with an accident.

In the Caribbean, poison was the preferred means of inflicting death, because the crime was difficult to detect. "Poison," said a Cuban slave implicated in the Conspiracy of the Ladder, "is better than warfare."[63] A Jamaican planter complained that the slaves' worst fault was "this prejudice respecting obeah, and the facility with which they are frequently induced to poison to the right and to the left."[64] Père Labat reported a slave's death-bed confession that he had killed more than thirty of his companions by poisoning them with the juice of a plant which grew along the seashore. The motive for his crime was that the master had shown favoritism to another slave.[65] A French colonial official proposed to offer freedom to slaves who revealed unknown poisons or poisoners, because of the loss of "a great number of whites, slaves, and cattle, dead of poisoning before one had, often before one could have, discovered the manner or the authors of these crimes; and because of the danger of communicating this secret from one area to another."[66]

In St. Domingue, fear of poisonings, imaginary or real, took on characteristics of mass hysteria during the last half of the eighteenth century. An intimate picture of the problem is revealed in the correspondence between the manager and the absentee owners of La Sucrerie Cottineau. By 1765, poison was killing both animals and slaves; among the latter, the *nègres sucriers*, the valuable, skilled slaves who had been slowly trained to carry out the delicate operations of the boiling house, were the main target. Thirty to forty of these slaves had presumably succumbed to poison within less than a decade. Animals were also being poisoned, and the manager was advised to check the nostrils of the work animals, since slaves killed

---

[62] *Loix*, Arrêt du Conseil de Léogane, August 1, 1707.

[63] Ortiz, *Los negros esclavos*, p. 434.

[64] Orlando Patterson, *The Sociology of Slavery: An Analysis of the Origin, Development, and Structure of Negro Slave Society in Jamaica* (New York: Humanities Press, 1969), p. 191.

[65] Père Jean-Baptiste Labat, *Nouveau voyage aux isles de l'Amèrique*, 2 vols. (Paris: Editions Duchartre, 1931), 2:68.

[66] Petit, *Gouvernement des esclaves*, vol. 2, pp. 75–76.

them by placing pointed sticks dipped in poison in their nostrils. The manager was instructed to use all means to discover who was supplying the poisons, and to "make an example capable of stopping such crimes," for the owners were certain of his justice and humanity. The poisoning of animals was stopped by making the slaves who took case of the animals responsible for their death.

The poisoning of slaves was a more intractable problem, and the search for the guilty parties continued. Even before a suspect was found, the owners found some satisfaction in speculating upon the punishment to be meted out. One owner favored "a private example" or summary justice on the spot. Another owner was for submitting the matter to the civil authorities for trial "if a conviction is certain." Others suggested bribing certain slaves for information. A suspect named Constant was seized, for the simple reason that he knew the work force best. The manager was advised to extract information from him, but not to kill him, since this would be a crime in the eyes of God. But, on the other hand, he could perhaps be made a severe example of before the entire plantation work force after the circumstances were explained to the general, the intendant, and the attorney general. Constant was executed on the plantation. Nevertheless, the poisonings continued, affecting not only La Sucrerie Cottineau, but the entire area of Fort-Dauphin. A slave named Jeannit from a neighboring plantation became the prime suspect. Jeannit had been a house slave who had been demoted to the field gang and then sold to the neighboing plantation, and the poisonings at La Sucrerie Cottineau were presumably his form of revenge. The owners suggested that the neighboring planters take up a subscription to compensate Jeannit's owner for his projected death. The manager filed a complaint against Jeannit with the civil authorities. Jeannit, two women slaves, Boukmann and her niece Marie-Louise who both belonged to La Sucrerie Cottineau, and Thomas, a slave from another estate, were tried before the civil authorities and all four were absolved because of the lack of proof. Nevertheless, Thomas was hanged by his master. La Dame Bauny, owner of a neighboring estate, executed five of her slaves as poisoners. Boukmann and Marie-Louise were returned to the estate. Their owners were resigned to Boukmann's death, since she was already forty-two years old, but not to Marie-Louise's, since she was only twenty-six and could still render service. Consequently, Boukmann was burned alive and Marie-Louise was placed in a dungeon, then released under careful surveillance. The manager of the estate that owned Jeannit, however, refused to execute him under his private authority. The owners of the neighboring estates were furious at this lapse of solidarity.

After the executions were over, the owners had second thoughts. A successful planter had told them that it was an "atrocious extremity" to grill men without trial, and one surely had no right to do so. It was, furthermore, the best way to reduce one's slaves to despair and to get one-self poisoned, or have one's throat cut by them. It was best to win their esteem by seeing to it that they lacked nothing. Instead of burning slaves alive, they suggested a *cachot affreux* (atrocious dungeon), and burning of the body *after* execution so the slave would not feel the pain. The nature of the poison was never made clear. And, in fact, after the burnings and the hangings, it was suspected that the deaths were really accidental, caused by the plumb used in the boiling house.[67]

POISON: REAL OR IMAGINARY?

It is not easy to evaluate the real extent of poisoning. To what degree was it a paranoid projection of the guilt and fear of the masters? To what extent was an African view accepted, that all sudden illness or death was due to sorcery which was intimately linked with the use of poisonous herbs?[68] During epidemics, would hysteria about poisoning not logically arise? Two competent contemporary observers conflict in their evaluations of the extent of poisonings perpetrated by the slaves of St. Domingue.

Hilliard d'Auberteuil believed that it was the ignorance and fear of the masters which caused them to attribute a ferocious character to their slaves. It was from the Europeans, he claimed, that slaves had learned the use of poison which had been fatal to so many people in the Dependance du Cap during the 1760s and 1770s. The source of the poison was not a secret, a sorcery or *ouanga*, as the people of the colony foolishly believed. It was not a vegetable poison, but came from the stock of a druggist that was sold after his death. A supply of arsenic and corrosive sublimate was

[67] This discussion of poisonings in Fort-Dauphin is based upon Gabriel Debien, *Plantations et esclaves à St. Domingue* (Dakar: Publications de la Section d'Histoire, Université de Dakar, 1962), pp. 61–68.

[68] E. E. Evans-Pritchard, *Witchcraft, Oracles and Magic among the Azande* (London: Oxford University Press, 1937), p. 397.

brought by a free black who was in league with Mackandal and who distributed it among the plantations. If the Africans had studied the use of poison in Guinea, they would have used it in other colonies like Jamaica where, Hilliard d'Auberteuil asserted, poisonings were very rare. Poisonings could be prevented by the careful policing of the pharmacies and by making the pharmacist responsible for the use made of the poisons in his stock. Hilliard d'Auberteuil claimed that there was only one vegetable poison in St. Domingue, the juice of the cane of Madera, which was very rare. There were several other vegetable poisons which affected cattle only. "Nevertheless, most whites live in fear, because they realize how much their slaves should hate them and take vengeance against them. Kind masters do not fear their slaves. Their slaves are their friends." [69]

Moreau de St.-Méry took a more somber view. The blacks, he said, believed in magic, and the power of their fetishes followed them across the seas. Many blacks acquired absolute power over their fellows by convincing them of their magical powers, and they obtained money, power, and sexual conquests by exploiting their belief in magic. Among the Africans sent to America, perhaps one-fourth were sold after being adjudged sorcerers. "Happy would be the part of the world where they are sent to expiate this crime, if poisoning, which is the cause of a great number of judgments of deportation, were just as imaginary." Although for a long time all the evils that could be explained by the climate and other physical causes were attributed to poisoners, nevertheless, "it is unfortunately all too true that the odious art of poisoning is profuse among the old Africans in St. Domingue. . . . Some of them have a school from which hatred and vengeance sends more than one disciple." [70]

The colonial authorities were impressed with the slaves' knowledge of unknown poisons. They carried out experiments upon a condemned poisoner, "in view of the multiple poisonings which devastate this part of the colony." The doctors attempted to discover the properties of natural poisons and their antidotes. They described a coma induced by the administra-

[69] Hilliard d'Auberteuil, *Considerations sur l'état présent de la colonie française de St. Domingue*, 2 vols. (Paris, 1776–77), 1:137–39.

[70] M. L. E. Moreau de St.-Méry, *Description topographique, physique, civile, politique, et historique de la partie française de l'Isle Saint-Domingue*, 4 vols. (Philadelphia, 1797), 1:56.

tion of a half ounce of a "grain common in America." The subject was revived by the use of certain unidentified drugs.[71]

HERBALISM IN AFRICA

Was this esoteric knowledge about herbs and their properties that colonial authorities attributed to the Africans a fiction? Information from present-day Africa confirms that Africans do, indeed, study the herbs of the forest, and do have an esoteric knowledge of the properties and uses of natural drugs and poisons. Shortly after World War II, Lieutenant von Staaten of the Basutoland Mounted Police seized a native drug called *maime* in connection with a ritual murder investigation. It was a Basuto chloroform administered to the victim to induce him to come along quietly. One whiff, and the victim acted like an automaton and was incapable of resistance. The drug had been unknown to the Europeans before this trial. In addition, Professor J. M. Watt of the Witwatersrand University was baffled by a laboratory test for poisonous properties of a tree bark used as evidence in the murder trial of a Zulu. The bark was boiled in water, but the extract proved inactive. The murder suspect volunteered the information that the bark had to be administered in powder form to secure results. The powder was deadly. It took five years to identify the tree from which the bark came. It was a species hitherto unknown to botanists. In Northern Rhodesia, members of the Ila tribe committed suicide by smoking the bark of the tree *Phyllanthus engleri*. Smoked slowly and carefully, it was medicinal. Deeply inhaled once or twice, it was fatal.[72]

An example of the use of drugs, hypnotism, and early socialization was the case of the Lion Men of Singida, Tanganyika, who killed over 200 people in 1920, and about 130 people in 1947. The police caught 57 suspects whom they charged with murder, 27 of whom were hanged. The Lion Men were adolescents under the control of contractors who ordered them to kill for a price. The Lion Men had been taken as small children, kept in cramped quarters, sometimes in bottles, their leg tendons cut to force them to walk on their hands and feet. They were kept drugged and hypnotized for years and were convinced that they were lions. They

[71] *Loix*, Arrêt du Conseil du Cap, April 8, 1758.
[72] Lawrence G. Green, *These Wonders to Behold* (Cape Town: The Standard Press Ltd., 1959), pp. 37–39.

73

struck their victims with clubs and clawed them with steel claws attached to their suits.[73]

It is clear, then, that the properties of herbs and their potentials in various realms of human relationships, especially in the realm of the impact of one mind upon another, is an ancient science in Africa. Much of the esoteric knowledge passed on from witchdoctors to their apprentices, as well as that passed on among destructive cults, relates to vegetable drugs, their preparation, properties, and uses.

Knowledge about herbs is considered personal property which can be sold to another person. This knowledge was widely distributed through sale throughout Africa because of the belief that the magic of a neighboring or distant tribe was always more powerful than one's own.[74] If it is true that many Africans were sold to the slave traders as punishment for sorcery, they would be well equipped, at least with techniques to investigate the properties of the plant life of the islands, if not with concrete knowledge of its flora. Much of the education and training of herbalists in Africa was creative, involving the investigation of new herbs. In a study of the training of sixteen witchdoctors among the Shona, all of whom used herbs, it was found that eleven were originally educated in their profession through dreams alone, without being trained by another herbalist.[75] This type of training necessarily implies a great deal of experimentation and creative work. The Africans' knowledge of herbs was certainly superior to that of the Europeans during the latter half of the eighteen century. In fact, the impact of chemicals upon the mind is only just beginning to attract the attention of Western investigators.

ATTEMPTS TO CONTROL THE SLAVES

It is clear that the slaves posed a real, not imaginary, threat to public order as well as to the very existence of the slave plantation colonies; the more plantation agriculture thrived and the more the slaves outnum-

---

[73] Alastair Scobie, *Murder for Magic: Witchcraft in Africa* (London: Cassell and Co., Ltd., 1965), pp. 139–42.

[74] Herskovits, *Dahomey*, vol. 1, pp. 78–95; Patterson, *Sociology of Slavery*, p. 183.

[75] Michael Gelfand, *The African Witch* (Edinburgh and London: E. and S. Livingstone, Ltd., 1967), p. 118.

bered the whites, the greater was the threat. How did the colonial authorities attempt to deal with this situation?

The problem of fugitive slaves was tackled from several angles. Savage punishments were inflicted upon them. Various forms of corporeal punishment, mutilation, and death became legal penalties for flight. The Cabildo of Havana suggested that the captured *cimarron*'s ear or nose be cut off, so that if he ran away again, he could be recognized.[76] Penalties for flight, ranging from flogging to death, were set forth in detail for the Spanish colonies in the mid-sixteenth century.[77] Cutting off ears and noses, and hamstringing were legal penalties for flight in St. Domingue. It was said that colonists resisted the penalty of hamstringing because they felt a "great repugnance at inflicting upon their slaves a punishment which would diminish their value."[78]

There were stringent punishments for aiding or harboring fugitive slaves. Slaves harboring fugitives were flogged, and free blacks faced the possibility of reenslavement, since in addition to being flogged, they had to pay the master for the time that his slave was away. If a free black could not raise the money, he risked being sold into slavery to cover these costs. On the complaint that free blacks were helping slaves to escape and receiving their stolen goods, causing "great disorder in the colony," the king of France ordered that any free black of St. Domingue found guilty of harboring a fugitive slave would be sold into slavery along with all the members of his family living with him.[79] As a result of this order, a free black named Hercule was sold into slavery for harboring fugitive slaves.[80]

Slave-hunting militias were formed early in Cuba. Before 1530 a *hermandad* of masters was organized to hunt fugitive slaves. Since this volunteer militia proved ineffective, professionalization set in. *Ranchadores* hunted down slaves for a price. Hunting dogs (*perras de busca*) were

---

[76] Rolando Mellafe, *La esclavitud en Hispano-américa* (Buenos Aires: Eudeba Editorial Universitaria de Buenos Aires, 1964), p. 83.

[77] Real Cédula, February 11, 1571, cited in Ortiz, *Los negros esclavos*, pp. 415–16.

[78] *Loix*, Ordonnance de M. de Galiffet, August 16, 1700.

[79] *DHFS*, vol. 1, pp. 237–40; Ortiz, *Los negros esclavos*, Appendix, pp. 444–48; *Loix*, Ordonnance du Roi, June 10, 1705; Arrêt du Conseil de Léogane, January 5, 1711; Edit du Roi, March, 1724; Déclaration du Roi, February 8, 1726.

[80] *Loix*, Arrêt du Conseil du Cap, March 23, 1768.

trained to hunt fugitive slaves. Fernando Ortiz reported that they were fed the flesh of slaves to make them more avid in the hunt. The *ranchadores* cut off the ears of their victims as physical evidence with which to claim a reward. Cuban-trained dogs were in demand throughout North America.[81] Militias were also organized in St. Domingue, where they proved as ineffective as in Cuba.[82] A permanent body of troops, the Maréchausée, was organized in 1717.[83] After an uneven career, during which it fell into neglect, the Maréchausée reorganized under pressing conditions. But the constant complaints about its ineffectiveness continued.[84]

Placing a price on the heads of fugitive slaves worked better. Slaves, free blacks and mulattoes, and professional bounty-hunters were actively engaged in the pursuit. In St. Domingue, for example, a price was put on the head of a fugitive slave named Noel, who "has assembled a considerable number of slaves around him, notably several foremen of different slave gangs, and he has succeeded in so frightening the colored people that they no longer dare present themselves before him."[85] Slaves were offered their freedom for capturing certain particularly troublesome leaders of maroon bands.[86] The French Crown opposed offering freedom to slaves for capturing leaders of maroon bands, because the result could be "great disorders in the colony from slaves who, to acquire this freedom, abandon labor on their masters' estates and arm themselves in groups under this pretext."[87] Cuban slaves were also active in the hunt for fugitives. Dr. Wurdemann reported: "The greatest number are captured by the slaves on the different estates, who obtain from the Captain of Partido $4.00 for each prisoner. . . . On a single estate where I resided, ten runaways were caught in a few months time by 3 or 4 negroes, who at their own request were permitted to patrol about the grounds after the last curfew."[88]

Rewards for the return of fugitive slaves became a corrupting influence undermining confidence in the professional slave-hunters. Complaints of

[81] Ortiz, *Los negros esclavos*, p. 399.

[82] *Loix*, Ordonnance des Administrateurs, August 14, 1717.

[83] *Loix*, Ordonnance des Administrateurs, March 27, 1721.

[84] *Loix*, Ordonnance des Administrateurs, January 20, 1733; Arrêt en Règlement du Conseil du Cap, August 6, 1739; Règlement du Roi, July 31, 1743.

[85] *Loix*, Arrêt du Conseil du Cap, March 27, 1775.

[86] *Loix*, Arrêt du Conseil de Léogane, May 4, 1716; Arrêt du Conseil du Petit-Goave, May 6, 1726.

[87] *Loix*, Arrêt du Conseil d'Etat, September 30, 1726.

[88] Wurdemann, *Notes on Cuba*, p. 262.

extortion came from all segments of society, the least protected suffering the most. The *ranchadores* of Cuba extorted money and other valuables from free blacks by threatening to hand them in as escaped slaves.[89] Members of the Maréchausée were accused of stopping slaves who were on legitimate business, tearing up their passes, and demanding rewards. The Maréchausée, however, claimed that unauthorized persons, impersonating members of the Maréchausée, were committing these offenses. The administrators ordered members of the Maréchausée to wear clear identification "so that they cannot accuse others of disorders of which they themselves are perfectly capable."[90]

The risk of betrayal among fugitive slaves was great. An early Spanish law offered freedom to the fugitive slave who voluntarily returned from the mountains bringing in another fugitive.[91] Esteban Montejo, a runaway Cuban slave, found it necessary to live completely alone in the mountains for ten years in order to avoid betrayal.[92] The promise of freedom and monetary rewards was probably more effective in undermining the fugitive slave colonies than the legal penalties against flight.

There were a number of laws enacted to ensure the general security of the colonies. Curfew laws, laws against assembly of slaves, pass laws, laws prohibiting slaves from owning arms and from riding horses, laws prohibiting the purchase of goods from a slave who did not have the written consent of his master: these were common measures in both St. Domingue and Cuba.[93] Exceptions were made for slaves working as cowboys, who were allowed to ride horses.[94] Slaves used for hunting, and trusted slaves were allowed to bear arms "to defend the slave quarters and protect food and cattle from incursions by fugitive slaves."[95] In St. Domingue, masters

[89] Ortiz, *Los negros esclavos*, pp. 399, 400.

[90] *Loix*, Ordonnance des Administrateurs, October 10, 1721.

[91] Ortiz, *Los negros esclavos*, p. 402.

[92] Esteban Montejo, *The Autobiography of a Runaway Slave*, ed. Miguel Barnet and trans. Jocasta Innes (New York: Random House, 1968).

[93] See Code Noir, Articles 18, 19, 35, and 36; *Loix*, Réglement de M. de Tracy, June 19, 1664; Arrêt du Conseil du Petit-Goave, January 8, 1697; Arrêt du Conseil du Cap, October 7, 1738; Arrêt du Conseil de la Martinique, June 13, 1658; Arrêt du Conseil du Cap, May 9, 1708; Ortiz, *Los negros esclavos*, pp. 346, 442, 444–48.

[94] Ortiz, *Los negros esclavos*, Appendix, pp. 444–48.

[95] *Loix*, Ordonnance des Administrateurs, July 1, 1717. See also Code Noir, Article 15.

were ordered to keep all arms and munitions under lock and key.[96] The death penalty was enacted for theft of arms by slaves.[97] The pass laws were ineffective, for many of the masters and overseers were illiterate. The signature of the master was rarely known by a colonist who might stop the slave, even if by chance he could read.[98]

Many laws were passed forbidding slaves and free blacks from handling drugs or working in pharmacies, the first example in St. Domingue dating from 1682.[99] A Royal Declaration dating from 1746 complained that slaves, using knowledge of certain plants and herbs, were poisoning other slaves and livestock, and enacted the death penalty for attempted poisoning. Slaves were not to compose or distribute any remedy in powder, or attempt to cure any sickness except for snakebite.[100] A slave was sentenced to be interrogated under torture and burned alive for having been found with a bowl of arsenic and for having poisoned more than 100 animals belonging to his master during an eight-month period of time.[101] After several slaves participated in a conspiracy to poison and then shoot their master at the instigation of their mistress,[102] laws against unauthorized persons handling drugs were extended to include the entire population.[103]

Enforcement of Security Measures

Enforcement of these security measures was sporadic. The authorities seemed to take comfort in trying to enforce them following emergency situations. After the execution of Mackandal, for example, police laws were expanded, codified, and published because the "almost complete lack of enforcement of these dispositions allowed disorders to persist, and necessarily

---

[96] *Loix*, Ordonnance des Administrateurs, Article 20, March 27, 1721.

[97] *Loix*, Déclaration du Roi, February 1, 1743.

[98] Petit, *Gouvernement des esclaves*, vol. 2, p. 155; Paul Trayer, *Etude historique de la condition des esclaves dans les colonies françaises* (Paris, 1887), p. 42.

[99] *Loix*, L'Edit de Juillet, 1682; Arrêt du Conseil du Cap, January 21, 1738; Arrêt en Règlement du Conseil du Cap, February 7, 1738; Ordonnance des Administrateurs concernant les Poisons, November 3, 1780; Arrêt du Conseil du Cap, contre un Apothecaire pour avoir vendu une Drogue Vénéneuse à un Nègre qui s'en est empoisonné, June 13, 1781; Arrêt du Conseil du Cap, qui renouvelle des défenses de laisser les Drogues et Médicamens entre les mains des Nègres.

[100] *Loix*, Déclaration du Roi, December 30, 1746.

[101] *Loix*, Arrêt du Conseil du Cap, December, 1777.

[102] *Loix*, Arrêt du Conseil de Léogane, July 18, 1738.

[103] *Ibid.*

reach a climax." [104] Again, in 1772, there was a note of sad resignation when the security laws were republished. "The preservation of order, a necessary result of wise police work, makes it necessary that the old regulations be put into effect once more in the City of Port-au-Prince, where the sickness of the times seems to have made them forgotten." [105]

The security laws did not effectively regulate the slave system. Yet, slave plantation societies managed to survive and function for a considerable length of time, pouring countless wealth into the hands of masters, slave traders, merchants, refiners, distributors, colonial officials, and most of all, the treasuries of the mother countries. How was order maintained on a sustained enough basis for these slave plantation societies to function? How were hundreds of slaves, who were being worked to death on isolated, rural estates and who were armed with machetes, convinced, for at least a significant length of time, not to murder their masters and overseers? On the most elementary level, the answer is that the person of the white had been made inviolate, and law had been effectively used as a means of establishing this principle. As early as the sixteenth century, special penalties were provided under Spanish law for any black, free or slave, who took up a weapon against a white, even if he did not use it. [106] The Code Noir provided the death penalty for the slave who struck his master, mistress, or their children and caused bruising or bleeding. [107] In St. Domingue, a slave was sentenced to be hanged for striking a white, the blow having resulted in the shedding of blood. [108] Several slaves were sentenced "to be broken alive and expire on the wheel, their heads placed on pikes along the highway" for having "defended themselves against a white" and having "wounded a white." [109] A free mulatto was sentenced to be flogged, branded, and sold into slavery for assaulting a white. [110] A French law provided that any colonist could shoot and kill any black whom he met at night who refused to stop when first commanded to do so. [111] Following a conspiracy, all blacks of Port-de-Paix were ordered to "behave respectfully towards whites, and the latter are authorized to kill them if they

---

[104] *Loix*, Arrêt en Règlement du Conseil du Cap, April 7, 1758.
[105] *Loix*, Ordonnance des Administrateurs, May 23, 1772.
[106] Ortiz, *Los negros esclavos*, p. 346.
[107] Article 33.
[108] *Loix*, Arrêt du Conseil du Cap, May 7, 1720.
[109] *Loix*, Arrêt du Conseil du Cap, October 2, 1777.
[110] *Loix*, Arrêt du Conseil du Port-au-Prince, January 22, 1767.
[111] *Loix*, Ordonnance des Administrateurs, Article 21, March 27, 1721.

perceive in their conduct the least sign of rebellion."[112] Hilliard d'Auberteuil wrote: "Negro slaves, and even freedmen of the colony, are menaced
by death if they dare defend themselves against a white, even after having
been assaulted. . . . In St. Domingue, any white can mistreat the blacks
with impunity. Their situation is such that they are slaves of their masters
and of the public."[113]

Savage legal penalties, including various forms of mutilation and slow
death under torture, were inflicted upon slaves in the Spanish colonies.[114]
Executions were public, and the heads of the executed slaves were com-
monly ordered to be exposed on pikes.[115] During the suppression of the
Conspiracy of the Ladder, the condemned were executed in the presence
of their fellow slaves on the estates where they had served.[116] In St.
Domingue, the executioner, called euphemistically the *Exécuteur des Hautes
Oeuvres* (Executioner of Exalted Works), was a slave who had been condemned to death and then offered his life in return for performing these
services. Many slaves preferred death when offered this choice.[117] On one
occasion, the executioner was murdered by the outraged crowd and the
condemned escaped.[118] In St. Domingue, there was a single judgment, by
no means atypical, against thirty slaves, men and women, black and mulatto,
which ordered "interrogation under ordinary and extraordinary torture . . .
hands cut off before the Church . . . drawn and quartered by four horses
. . , their members thrown into the fire, their ashes to the wind . . . heads
exposed on pikes. . . ."[119]

Was all this savagery really necessary? Given the insecurity of the system, the rebelliousness of the slaves, the relative ineffectiveness of both
legal security measures and methods of socialization such as religious conversion and indoctrination, it appears that paralyzing the hand that might
strike down the master through the most naked forms of terror was the
cement that held the system together.

[112] *Loix*, Ordre concernant les Nègres de la Dépendance du Cap, November 12,
1691.
[113] Hilliard d'Auberteuil, *Considerations sur l'état*, vol. 1, p. 145.
[114] Mellafe, *Esclavitud en Hispano-américa*, p. 83.
[115] *Loix*, Ordonnance des Administrateurs, Article 8, May 27, 1721.
[116] *Fallos*.
[117] *Loix*, Arrêt du Conseil du Petit-Goave, May 6, 1726.
[118] *Loix*, Arrêt du Conseil du Cap, March 15, 1717.
[119] *Loix*, Arrêt du Conseil du Petit-Goave, May 6, 1726.

V

PROTECTIVE ASPECTS OF
SLAVE LAW

T HE MOTHER COUNTRIES played the major role in formulating the slave laws of both St. Domingue and Cuba. Protective aspects of these laws as well as security measures, can be understood only within the context of the role which the metropolis attempted to play in looking out for the long-range interests of the slave system as a major source of wealth for the metropolis. The basic objectives of slave law were to preserve order in the colony, maintain and develop its wealth, and continue its dependency upon the mother country so that the colony would continue to play the role ordained by the metropolis. In a flourishing slave plantation society, these long-range aims often came into conflict with the plantation owners' drive for immediate profit. This drive was especially acute among absentee owners and their managers and among colonists who planned to make as much money as they could as soon as possible and then return to Europe. The main concern of slave law, including its protective aspects, was social control in a broad sense. Those measures which tended toward protecting the slaves cannot be understood simply as indications of the disinterested humanitarianism of the colonizing powers. Rather, they reflect concern about the threat to public order and to the continued exis- tence of the colony posed by the slaves and the desire to preserve the slave work force as the price of slaves rose on the African coasts and as inter- national opposition to the African slave trade became a serious threat to the continuance of the trade. It is clear from certain documents that moral considerations often read into texts of slave law by defenders of the slave system and by contemporary comparative historians were at best incidental.

A Spanish slave code of the Bourbon Reform period, the Código Negro Carolino, pointed out that the blacks in the colony far outnumbered the whites, and were

. . . violently extracted from their country and family, reduced to slavery, and deprived of liberty; their robust bodies are accustomed to intemperance, and their strong limbs are constantly armed, even for the very labor of the field. [Laws should be formulated] that keep constantly in mind the events created by their compatriots in the colonies of Surinam, Jamaica, and Martinique, and formerly in the Island of Hispaniola.

This Code called for leading the slaves

by the solid principles of education, which is the most delicate and important resort of police and justice, the most severe discipline and force being incapable by itself of containing them from excesses of sedition and flight which the inaccessibility of the mountains makes convenient.[1]

Laws requiring masters to feed their slaves and regulating the punishments that the masters could inflict were motivated by the desire to control theft and discourage the slaves from running away. A memorandum of two governors of the French West Indies which was used by Colbert in preparing the Code Noir of 1685 stated, "It is necessary to insist that the plantation owners feed them. Otherwise they will steal from the small owners and become runaways."[2] Emilien Petit, a high colonial official in late eighteenth-century France, wrote that there would be "inhumanity and danger" in failing to require that masters feed their slaves.

Slaves who do not find food on the land where they live are forced to go out and look for it, pilfering the provisions of the neighbors, or stealing to procure it, which results in the greatest difficulty in conserving the slave and maintaining the safety of the neighborhood, or even of the colony, by the opportunities thus afforded for deserting and joining with other deserted slaves.[3]

[1] C.N.C., Preamble.
[2] Lucien Peytraud, *L'Esclavage aux antilles françaises avant 1789* (Paris, 1897), p. 154.
[3] Emilient Petit, *Traité sur le gouvernement des esclaves*, 2 vols. (Paris: Knapen, 1777), 2:122–28.

An Ordonnance du Roi dating from 1712 complained that the

subjects of the French islands of America do not feed their slaves, and under various pretexts make them suffer, under their own authority, interrogation under torture with a cruelty unknown, even among the most barbarous nations; so that these slaves are for a long time incapable of rendering any service, and there are even some who remain maimed; and those who have not yet been subjected to such punishments, intimidated by the example, become deserters to avoid such inhumanity, which causes a great disorder in the said islands.[4]

Hilliard d'Auberteuil suggested that, to discourage flight, "it is necessary to give them wives, encourage them to raise cattle, hold them with the ties of property. They must be put into the position where they cannot easily do without their masters."

As soon as a slave can meet his own needs, he is no longer dependent, and nature reasserts its rights. She frees him from the yoke under which he was oppressed, and renders vain the law of the strong. How contain a slave who has no needs? Who owns nothing? In vain will his master avail himself of superior strength to force him to obey, to work, to stay with him. He must redouble his vigilance, so that he does not lose sight of him for a moment. He must shut him up in a well-locked place, for fear that he will escape or that he will kill himself if he cannot escape. If his severity, his tyranny, relaxes for a moment, the slave reaches the woods and his chains are broken.[5]

There were, then, clearly practical motives for trying to prevent excesses by slaveowners which, by exasperating the slaves, could jeopardize public order or even the continued existence of the colony.

Protective aspects of slave law can be interpreted as stated policy. The degree of interest exhibited by the colonizing powers in enforcing these measures can best be studied through case law and other attempts to implement the law. There was a sharp conflict between the broad considerations of social control motivating the metropolis and the immediate interests of the individual planters, who insisted upon exploiting their human property without outside restraint and demanded that they remain the sole authority in the eyes of their slaves. The gap between theory and practice

[4] *Loix*, Ordonnance du Roi, December 30, 1712.
[5] Hilliard d'Auberteuil, *Considerations sur l'état présent de la colonie française de St. Domingue*, 2 vols. (Paris, 1776–77), 2:59–62.

in both St. Domingue and Cuba was enormous. There was, however, a significant contrast between the two colonies. Spanish law was vague, abstract, and self-righteous in style, and attempts to enforce it were weak. French law was concrete and practical; it contained few moralistic trappings; and attempts at enforcement were serious and persistent, although largely unsuccessful.

THE FRENCH SYSTEM

The Code Noir, promulgated in 1685, was a complete slave code based upon Roman slave law and formulated with American conditions in mind, officials familiar with these conditions having been consulted during the formulation of the code. Protective aspects of the Code Noir are impressive, especially considering the date it was formulated. For example, the master was ordered to furnish the following items each week to slaves aged ten years or over: two and a half *pots* of manioc flour, or three cassavas weighing at least two and a half pounds each, or equivalent items, as well as two pounds of salt beef, or three pounds of fish, or other proportionate foods, and half rations for children under ten. Rum could not be substituted for the above articles; nor could the master permit the slave to work for himself one day a week instead of furnishing nourishment and subsistence. Each slave had to be given either two suits of clothes or four measures of cloth each year. Neglected or mistreated slaves could complain to the *procureur general*. Disabled slaves, whether incurable or not, had to be maintained by the master.[6]

There is evidence that the authorities in St. Domingue tried seriously to enforce these measures. In 1706, the Conseil de Léogane and the Conseil du Cap took vigorous action, explaining that

all orders previously given to force the colonists to have the necessary food for the subsistence of their Negroes, as well as to prevent all accidents which can arise in this colony, have been impossible to enforce, and one sees daily accidents arising, and Negroes becoming fugitives because of lack of food, and others found dead or maimed while stealing food from the near neighbors of their masters.

It was ordered that within two months, 150 feet of manioc and 10 feet of bananas had to be planted for each Negro over the age of 12 and under the

[6] Articles 22, 23, 24, 25, 26, and 27.

age of 60. Every year, one barrel of grain, peas, maize, or flour was to be furnished for each slave; this stipulation, however, was not to result in a decrease of the amount of crops, such as potatoes or yams, that was usually planted. A fine was to be imposed for violation.[7] Resistance from the planters was strong, but so was the determination of the colonial authorities. Two sheriffs (*huissiers*) who had "neglected" to publish the orders in several parishes were fined for their "neglect" and instructed to publish the order.[8] The following year, it was reported that the order had been only partially complied with. An inspection system was set up to ensure that the quantity of food prescribed by the orders had actually been planted.[9] Provision was also made for verifying the claims of fugitives slaves that they had deserted because of lack of food.[10]

The Code Noir contained safeguards against brutalization of slaves; it severely restricted the master's right to punish except for minor disciplinary matters, and in such cases, restricted the type and quantity of punishment the master was entitled to inflict. Slaves who had committed offenses warranting severe punishment were to receive court trials.

. . . the slaves shall be accused, judged in the first instance by ordinary judges, and by appeal to the Sovereign Council, with the same instructions and with the same formalities as for free persons. . . . Masters can, when they believe that their slaves have merited it, chain them and have them beaten with a switch or a rope. They cannot be tortured, nor can any of their members be mutilated, under penalty of confiscation of the slaves and being proceeded against extraordinarily. . . . We order our officers to pursue criminally the masters or commanders who have killed a slave under their power or their direction, and to punish the murder according to the atrocity of the circumstances.[11]

Judgments against masters for mutilating slaves predate the Code Noir. A judgment dating from 1670 broke a lieutenant of the militia to the ranks because "he vexed his wife and mutilated his Negroes."[12] Another early judgment fined a master 500 livres of sugar and threatened corporal

[7] *Loix*, Règlement du Conseil de Léogane, May 3, 1706; Arrêt du Conseil du Cap, June 7, 1706. See also Règlement du Roi, August 26, 1721.
[8] *Loix*, Arrêt du Conseil de Léogane, October 11, 1706.
[9] *Loix*, Arrêt du Conseil du Cap, March 14, 1707.
[10] *Loix*, Arrêt du Conseil de Léogane, March 11, 1726.
[11] Articles 32, 42, and 43.
[12] *Loix*, Arrêt du Conseil de la Martinique, October 20, 1670.

punishment if he repeated the offense. He had struck his slave several times with a lash, wounding her seriously in several parts of her body, and "burning her private parts with a hot poker."[13] After the promulgation of the Code Noir, several judgments appeared against masters and overseers for brutalizing slaves. A white commander was fined for inflicting punishment resulting in a slave's death.[14] A manager was permanently banished from the colony for having "in an excess of violence killed with a rifle shot the Negro Pompee who belonged to his employer."[15] A fugitive slave was absolved because of the treatment he had received at the hands of the master. According to Moreau de St.-Méry, this was a common procedure.[16] Masters were reminded that they could not give slaves *la question* under any pretext, under penalty of a 500 livres fine, and when slaves had committed any crime, the *juges ordinaires* were to proceed against them, in accordance with the law.[17]

Although there were examples of action against overseers and managers and against a free colored person who had killed his slave,[18] it is clear that the authorities hesitated to act against wealthy and powerful masters. The contrast between the punishment and the crime is evident in the case of M. St. Martin, a colonist from Artibonite, described by the administrator as "a man of great fortune, fortune which would be even greater if he had not himself diminished it by his inhumanity." M. St. Martin had killed more than 200 of his slaves, the last five or six perishing from "total mutilation." The Minister of the Marine wrote that he had received many complaints about mistreatment of slaves in St. Domingue and had thought them to be exaggerated, but after this case, "it gives me great pain to see that there was not as much exaggeration as I had thought." M. St. Martin was fined 150,000 livres, but retained the 300 or 400 slaves he still owned.[19]

[13] *Loix*, Arrêt du Conseil de la Martinique, May 10, 1671.
[14] *Loix*, Arrêt du Conseil du Cap, July 2, 1715.
[15] *Loix*, Arrêt du Conseil du Cap, May 6, 1746.
[16] *Loix*, Arrêt du Conseil du Cap, May 8, 1714.
[17] *Loix*, Ordonnance du Roi, December 30, 1712.
[18] *Loix*, Arrêt du Conseil du Port-au-Prince, October 26, 1784.
[19] Lettre du Administrateur de St. Domingue au Ministre, March 28, 1741, A.N. Colonies, F³ 143, pp. 100–103, cited in Antoine Gisler, *L'Esclavage aux antilles françaises (XVIIe–XIXe siècles): Contribution au problème de l'esclavage* (Fribourg: Editions Universitaires Fribourg Suisse, 1964), p. 107; *Loix*, Lettre du Ministre à M. M. de Larnage et Maillart, July 25, 1741.

Hilliard d'Auberteuil believed that protective laws had little impact on the colonists. The protective laws "do not prevent Negroes from perishing daily in chains, or under the lash; from being smothered, strangled, burned up without any kind of trial. . . . Many cruelties still go unpunished."[20] During the last few decades of the colony, when fear of poisoners gripped the masters, slaves suspected of being poisoners were tortured and burned alive, and forced to reveal the names of their accomplices, real or imaginary. Those named were in turn tortured and burned alive. Efforts by the metropolis to punish masters committing these atrocities crumbled in the face of the solidarity of the planter class.[21]

French law attempted to regulate the amount of labor exacted from the slaves. During the early years of the colony, masters were not to demand labor from slaves on Sundays and holidays.[22] Under the Code Noir, slaves were not to be worked from midnight to midnight on Sundays and holidays, under penalty of confiscation of the sugar as well as of the slaves caught working during these hours.[23] Since "renters are not at all responsible for the mortality of slaves and they wear them out with excessive labor, nourish them very badly, and give no care during their illnesses, which has caused the death of several," an Ordonnance du Roi dating from 1711 attempted to protect rented slaves from excess labor by making the lessee civilly responsible for their death, and in recompense, allowing him to keep children born of rented slaves.[24] Provisions of the Code Noir regulating work hours were reiterated on several occasions.[25]

The French Crown made a serious effort to maintain normal court procedures in criminal complaints against slaves, even in emergency situations. The governor of the colony, for example, was severely reprimanded for violating normal court procedures in suppressing the Conspiracy of 1691. "[His Majesty] has found the execution carried out by M. de la Boulais of several Negroes who had formed the plan of going over to the enemy

---

[20] Hilliard d'Auberteuil, *Considerations sur l'état*, vol. 1, p. 144.
[21] The LeJeune case represented the triumph of the planters over attempts by the metropolis to interfere with the slave regime. See C. L. R. James, *The Black Jacobins*, 2d ed. rev. (New York: Vintage Books, 1963), pp. 22–24.
[22] *Loix*, Arrêt du Conseil de la Martinique, October 7, 1692.
[23] Article 6.
[24] *Loix*, Ordonnance du Roi, April 20, 1711.
[25] *Loix*, Ordonnance du Juge de St. Marc, November 26, 1726.

too military and irregular, and he recommends that you pay particular attention in the future to avoid these kinds of procedures."[26] The metropolitan authorities protested the violation of the provisions of the Code Noir which made mandatory an appeal to the higher court in all criminal cases involving slaves. "One should not, under any circumstances, introduce usages which tend to undermine the execution of the *Ordonnances*. When experience shows that there are inconveniences in executing them, one can point this out, and propose means for remedying the situation."[27] In 1741, the king ordered suspension of all sentences to the galleys and death penalties for desertion of slaves, and each case was to be reported to the administrators of the colonies.[28] Attempts to cover up irregular procedures in criminal trials of slaves might have inspired two separate orders to burn the records of such trials.[29]

We have, however, an example of exemplary punishment and suspension of normal procedures. The master filed a formal complaint, and the Captain of Militia denounced twenty-one slaves, men and women with baggage, five of them armed, who were preparing to desert to the Spanish. The order explained that because of frequent disorders arising from the desertion and rebellion of the Negroes Alexandre and Cesar, two of the leaders of the gang held, they were to be tried and hanged on the spot without further procedure, and their heads were to be placed on pickets on the estate.[30] It is clear, however, that while normal procedures were violated by the colonial authorities, the metropolis did not authorize such violations and attempted to prevent them.

Although France developed a slave system in America without a long tradition of slavery and slave law, the thoroughness and practicality of the French slave code, the concreteness of its protective measures, the early

[26] *Loix*, Lettre du Ministre à M. Ducasse, August 27, 1692.

[27] *Loix*, Lettre du Ministre à M. Methon (Covering letter for Ordonnance du Roi, April 20, 1711). The Ordonnance du Roi stated that since there were more black slaves in the colony since the promulgation of the Code Noir, more crimes were committed, and since it took too long to appeal all of the sentences to the Conseil Supérieur, such appeal was mandatory thereafter only for sentences of death or hamstringing. Other penalties were to be judged in the last resort by the *juges ordinaires*.

[28] *Loix*, Ordre des Administrateurs aux Procureurs-Généraux, November 21, 1741.

[29] *Loix*, Arrêt du Conseil de Léogane, January 4, 1717; Arrêt du Conseil du Cap, July 3, 1724.

[30] *Loix*, Arrêt du Conseil du Cap, September 22, 1721.

date of its promulgation, and the seriousness with which the metropolis attempted to enforce it are impressive. The contrast with Spanish slave law in these respects is sharp.

SPANISH SLAVE LAW BEFORE THE BOURBON REFORMS

In theory, slavery in the Spanish colonies developed within the framework of existing Spanish slave law. The Siete Partidas del Rey Alfonso el Sabio was a slave code dating from the thirteenth century. It addressed itself to the problems of a domestic slave system and had little relevance to American conditions. Spanish slave law in America developed haphazardly and was mainly concerned with security measures. Response to the problem of protection of slaves was very slow and abstract. When attempts were finally made during the 1780s to create a Spanish slave code, protective measures were based primarily upon French slave law.

Ordenanzas formulated for Cuba in 1574 indicated that inadequate care and excessive punishment of slaves were creating serious control problems. Slaves who were not provided for by their masters were attacking "neighboring farms in order to eat, and because of such bad treatment, they revolt and become fugitives." Masters were

flogging them with great cruelty, larding them with different types of resins, broiling them, and committing other cruelties from which they die or remain so afflicted and maimed that they kill themselves or throw themselves into the sea, or run away, or revolt, and those who say that they have killed their slaves are not proceeded against.

While these *ordenanzas* set up, in theory, an inspection system to see that slaves were not neglected or mistreated, they were not promulgated until seventy years after they were formulated.[31]

The vagueness of Spanish law is evident from a Real Cédula dating from 1683. Complaining that Negro and mulatto slaves were dying from excessive punishments and that slaves were being inadequately fed and clothed, the king called for the forced sale of the slaves in proven instances of continued mistreatment, "if the case calls for it." But no restriction was placed upon the type or amount of punishment the master could inflict,

[31] Ordenanzas de Alonso de Cáceres, Nos. 60 and 61, promulgated April 26, 1641; Fernando Ortiz, *La hampa afro-cubana: Los negros esclavos* (Havana: Ruiz y Cª, 1916), Appendix, pp. 444–48.

nor were procedures established for civil trials of slaves accused of serious offenses.[32]

In fact, the Crown pronounced against holding ordinary criminal trials of fugitive slaves involved in "mutinies, seditions and rebellion [who carried] out uprisings," and of slaves who were "infamous thieves." The leaders were ordered to be punished exemplarily, and the rest reduced to slavery and service "because their condition is that of slaves and fugitives from their masters, making for justice in the matter and excusing time and trial."[33]

The Street Slaves

One example of the contrast between the vagueness of Spanish law and the concreteness of French law was the manner in which the problem of street slaves was handled. It was a common practice throughout the Americas to allow certain slaves to work for themselves in return for bringing the master a fixed sum of money. If the slave was skilled and the money demanded by the master was not excessive, the arrangement was advantageous to the slave, allowing him to dispose of his own time and opening up the possibility of self-purchase. Unskilled slaves were often forced into excessive labor, theft, and prostitution to secure the sums of money demanded by their masters. Street slaves were prevalent in port cities.

In Brazil, street slaves were used as pack animals to carry 200-pound loads on their heads. Gilberto Freyre estimated the life expectancy of the Brazilian street slave at seven years.[34] The Portuguese Crown felt called upon to condemn as "particularly shameful the practice of lady owners living on the immoral earnings of their female slaves, who were not merely encouraged but forced into a life of prostitution."[35]

The authorities of St. Domingue believed that controlling street slaves and restricting self-purchase were essential in controlling crime in the colony. They concluded that the high crime rate resulted from the "avidity of several colonists who, with no other motives except their avarice, place

[32] *DHFS*, Real Cédula, October 12, 1683, vol. 2, p. 754.

[33] Real Cédula, September 14, 1619, cited in Ortiz, *Los negros esclavos*, pp. 419–20.

[34] Gilberto Freyre, *The Mansions and the Shanties* (New York: Alfred A. Knopf, 1963), pp. 311, 312.

[35] C. R. Boxer, *The Golden Age of Brazil* (Berkeley and Los Angeles: University of California Press, 1962), pp. 138, 140.

a money price upon the liberty of their Negro slaves, which brings them to use the most illicit means for procuring the necessary sums for obtaining this liberty. . . ." [36] Street slaves were outlawed in St. Domingue, and any slave allowed by his master to work for himself was ordered to be arrested.[37] Masters were not to allow their slaves to be engaged in any business for their own account, nor to let them wander about as vagabonds and hire as they pleased in return for either a daily or monthly sum of money, under penalty of fine for the first offense and confiscation of the slave for the second.[38] When a slave who had been allowed to work for himself was executed, his master was deprived of the price that he would have ordinarily received for an executed slave.[39]

Forced prostitution was a problem in the Spanish colonies as well. A Real Cédula dating from 1672 forbade masters from sending their female slaves or free black women out as street vendors, for "if they do not bring back the profits which they suppose they should, they send them out at night to whatever torpor and dishonesty leads them to." [40] A Real Cédula of 1710 commented upon "the scandalous abuse of sending Negro and mulatto women out to earn a daily sum, most of them going out in public nude, with notable scandal, and going over to committing many mortal sins in order to bring to their masters the customary amount." The police were ordered to return such slaves to their masters when they were found in the streets. The bishops and archbishops were called upon to make exhortations and representations to prevent such scandals, and the governors were instructed to see that when mistreatment against slaves could be proved the slaves were sold.[41] The Real Cédula of 1693 addressed to the governor of Havana, parts of which are often cited to prove the mildness of slavery in the Spanish Empire,[42] was actually a vague pronouncement in lieu of concrete action when the problem of forced prostitution of slaves

---

[36] Loix, Ordonnance du Roi, April 11, 1713.

[37] Loix, Ordonnance du Juge de Police du Cap, September 17, 1762.

[38] Loix, Arrêt du Conseil du Port-au-Prince, February 11, 1785.

[39] Some examples are Loix, Arrêt du Conseil du Cap, May 15, 1772; Arrêt du Conseil du Port-au-Prince, February 11, 1785.

[40] DHFS, vol. 2, p. 589.

[41] DHFS, vol. 3, p. 113.

[42] See Frank Tannenbaum, Slave and Citizen: The Negro in the Americas (New York: Alfred A. Knopf, 1946), p. 89; Stanley M. Elkins, Slavery: A Problem in American Institutional and Intellectual Life (Chicago: University of Chicago Press, 1959), p. 68; Herbert S. Klein, Slavery in the Americas: A Comparative Study of Virginia and Cuba (Chicago: University of Chicago Press, 1967), p. 76.

was called to the attention of the Crown. After studying the amount of money exacted daily by the masters of street slaves, the Crown decided against regulating the amount and opted for exhortation instead.

Call together the masters of said slaves and tell them in my name that for no motive should they rigorously increase this daily sum, because doing so in several places has resulted in various inconveniences with danger to the souls of these people, a matter of grave scruple, and for the sake of their own consciences the masters should avoid it.[43]

It was not until the Bourbon Reform period that attempts were made to regulate street slaves under Spanish law. The Código Negro Español outlawed female street slaves.[44] The Código Negro Carolino outlawed all street slaves, except those exploited for the support of "poverty-stricken persons, such as minors, widows, and old people."[45]

Marriage and the Family

French slave law showed early concern with promoting marriage among the slaves. A law dating from 1664 provided that masters must see to the baptism of Negroes who get off the ships, to their marriage, and to the baptism of the children of said marriages, under penalty of fine, or forced sale of the slaves "to be put into more Christian hands."[46] Dutertre reported that marriage was encouraged, and it was customary to purchase the marriage partner so that the couple could live together on the same estate.[47] The Code Noir provided for marriage of slaves with the consent of the master. Masters could not force slaves to marry against their will.[48] There is evidence that slave marriage was taken seriously, at least during the early years of the colony. In 1715, the king pardoned a slave who had murdered his adulterous wife.[49]

French law was concretely and unequivocally protective of the slave family. The Code Noir provided

---

[43] *DHFS*, vol. 3, p. 40.

[44] Cap. 3.

[45] Cap. 50 and 51.

[46] *Loix*, Règlement de M. de Tracy, June 19, 1664.

[47] Jean-Baptiste Dutertre, *Hoistoire générale des antilles habitées par les françois*, 4 vols. (Paris, 1667–71), 2:504–5.

[48] Articles 10 and 11.

[49] *Loix*, Arrêt du Conseil du Cap, January 2, 1715.

The husband, wife, and their children under the age of puberty [interpreted as 14 years old] cannot be seized and sold separately, if they are all under the power of the same master. We declare void all separate seizures and sales which shall be made. The penalty against those who have made voluntary alienations is to be deprived of the one or ones he has kept, who will be adjudged to the acquirers, without their having to pay any supplement in price.[50]

Indications are that these provisions were effectively enforced. Charlevoix reported that masters discouraged marriage among their slaves because "the Law of the Prince, as well as that of the Church, forbids them to sell the husband without the wife and their children under a certain age."[51] During the late colonial period, Hilliard d'Auberteuil wrote, "It is neither permitted nor possible to sell Negro children separately from their mothers."

. . . in the leasing of Negroes the lessee is responsible for their death, and consequently, the Negro children born during the course of the lease belong to him; but since they cannot be separated from their mother, their owner takes them at the termination of the lease, and compensates the lessee in accordance with the estimate of their value made when they are turned over to him.[52]

Legal protection of the slave family under French law survived in the state of Louisiana even after it became a part of the United States.

While slave marriage and the slave family were recognized and protected under French law, indications are that marriage was resisted, not only by the masters, but also by the slaves. "The blacks on their side," wrote Charlevoix, "are never in a hurry to marry, because they view this second involvement as a kind of servitude even more onerous than that into which they are born."[53]

Early Spanish law offered considerably less protection to the slave family, although marriage among slaves was encouraged. Masters were reassured that marriage would free neither the slaves nor the children they might have. Slaves could marry each other; they could marry a free

---

[50] Article 47.
[51] Père Pierre-François-Xavier de Charlevoix, *Histoire de l'Isle espagnole ou St. Domingue* (Paris, 1731), p. 505.
[52] Hilliard d'Auberteuil, *Considérations sur l'état*, vol. 2, pp. 65, 66 n.
[53] Charlevoix, *Histoire de St. Domingue*, p. 505.

person if the latter knew they were slaves; but only Christians could marry. Consent of the master was not necessary if the slave continued to serve the master. The master could not sell a husband and wife separately if it would mean they would not be able to live together. If the master knew of a marriage between his slave and a free person and failed to report that he was a slave, the slave became free.[54] No Negro slave married in the Spanish Kingdom could be brought to America without his wife and children.[55]

During the early sixteenth century, the Crown took vigorous measures to encourage marriage among slaves. An equal number of male and females slaves were to be brought to Española, and those slaves who were not married within fifteen months were to be subject to a special tax. Concern for social stability and public order motivated the Spanish Crown to encourage marriage among slaves. A measure dating from 1527 explained the practical side of this concern.

. . . many Negroes have gone to Española, each day many more go, and few Spanish Christians are there. This could be a cause of some unrest or uprising of the said Negroes. [Since groups of slaves] flee from the estates and haciendas and go to the mountains . . . there is no security. [With that and] with the possibility of other dangers and inconveniences . . . it seems that it would be a great remedy to have the Negroes married who, from this time forward, go to the said island and to have those [men] already there married. The love that they feel for their wives and children and the order of matrimony would calm them down and they would avoid other sins and inconveniences.[56]

None of these early measures prohibited the separation of a mother and her child if he was a minor, through sale or seizure. While Spanish law continued to reflect concern about promoting marriage and procreation among slaves, concern about separation of mother and child remained weak throughout the history of slavery in the Spanish colonies. During the Bourbon Reform period, when marriage and procreation were considered "urgent to prevent flight and compensate for the scarcity noted on the coasts of Guinea,"[57] the provisions against separation of families re-

---

[54] *DHFS*, Real Provision, May 11, 1526, vol. 1, p. 81.
[55] *DHFS*, Real Cédula, February 1, 1570, vol. 1, p. 451.
[56] *DHFS*, Real Provision of 1527, vol. 1, pp. 99, 100.
[57] C.N.C., Cap. 25 and 146.

mained weak. Married slaves could not be sold or embarked separately, nor the wife without the husband and their children, "if no prejudice to a third party followed [*a no seguirse perjuicio de tercero*]."[58] This provision did not protect the slave family from separation in cases of forced sale or seizure, during the division of an estate, or under any circumstances where the master could establish that he would be injured by keeping the slave family intact. The Código Negro Español was even weaker. Masters could not prevent the marriage of their slaves with those belonging to others and were obliged to purchase the marriage partner, but there was no prohibition against separation of mother and child. Even in the case of the purchase of the wife, there was no obligation to purchase the children which she might already have.[59] An 1842 Cuban code contained a very limited prohibition against selling children separately from their mother. When the master of the husband bought the wife, he was also obliged to buy the children under the age of three years which she might already have.[60] Aside from the very low age limit, there was no prohibition against the separate sale of mother or child when no new marriage was involved, nor against seizure of children, who were minors, for debt, nor against separation of mother and child while an estate was being settled.

Small children were freely sold in Cuba. Fernando Ortiz wrote that it was even normal to sell pregnant and nursing slaves, with or without their infants, and slaves were sold apart from their mothers and before their birth for twenty-five pesos. Eight days after the birth of the child, the price went up to fifty pesos. A newspaper contained the following ad: "For sale, a 26-year old *mulata*, married in the Villa of Santiago, with her 5-month old infant, 300 pesos. Infant not included."[61] Esteban Montejo, a slave born in Cuba, wrote that he never knew his parents. He had never seen them. "Blacks were sold like pigs, and they sold me at once, which is why I remember nothing about the place."[62] Here is his description of the child care arrangements on Cuban estates.

[58] C.N.C., Cap. 129.
[59] C.N.E., Cap. 7.
[60] Bando de Gobernación y Policía de la Isla de Cuba, por el Capitan Sr. D. Gerónimo Valdès, November 14, 1842, and Reglamento de esclavos y Instrucciones de Pedaneos, Article 31, in Ortiz, *Los negros esclavos*, Appendix, pp. 482–97.
[61] *Papel Periódo de la Habana*, 1790, cited in Ortiz, *Los negros esclavos*, p. 175.
[62] Esteban Montejo, *The Autobiography of a Runaway Slave*, ed. Miguel Barnet and trans. Jocasta Innes (New York: Random House, 1968), p. 14.

All the plantations had an infirmary near the barracoon, a big wooden hut where they took the pregnant women. You were born there and stayed there till you were 6 or 7, when you went to live in the barracoons and began work, like the rest. There were Negro wet-nurses and cooks there to look after the *criollitos* and feed them. . . . Sometimes a *criollito* never saw his parents again because the boss moved them to another plantation, and so the wet-nurses would be in sole charge of the child. But who wants to bother with another person's child? [63]

Montejo described slave breeding:

A child of good stock cost 500 pesos, that is the child of strong, tall parents. Tall Negroes were privileged. The masters picked them out to mate them with tall, healthy women and shut them up together in the barracoon and forced them to sleep together. The women had to produce healthy babies every year. I tell you, it was like breeding animals. Well, if the Negress didn't produce as expected, the couple were separated and she was sent to work in the fields again. Women who were barren were unlucky because they had to go back to being beasts of burden again, but they were allowed to choose their own husbands. [64]

Montejo was describing conditions in Cuba during the late nineteenth century, when the slave trade had actually ended. But slave-breeding was also reported from Cartagena in 1752.[65] It is evident that protection of the slave family was unimpressive in the Spanish colonies, either in law or in practice.

THE BOURBON REFORM PERIOD

During the last two decades of the eighteenth century, serious efforts were undertaken to reform the slave law and the slave systems in the Caribbean. All of the colonies, British, French, and Spanish, were involved. While these efforts are often interpreted as stemming from the humanitarianism engendered by the Enlightenment, the matter is much more complex. The principle of free trade was, among all the other aspects of enlighten-

---

[63] *Ibid.*, p. 38.

[64] *Ibid.*, p. 39. Moreno Fraginals lists the following slave-breeding farms in Cuba during the 1850s and 1860s: that of José Suarez Argudín near the Playa of Bacuranao; that of Tomás Teruz of Cienfuegos; that of Esteban Santa Cruz de Oviedo, the *ingenio* Trinidad. Manuel Moreno Fraginals, *El ingenio: El complejo económico social cubano del azucar* (Havana: Comisión Nacional Cubana de la UNESCO, 1964), p. 156.

[65] *DHFS*, vol. 3, p. 260.

ment thought, most attractive to the planter classes in the Caribbean. The American Revolution set off a chain reaction which shook the Caribbean colonies to their foundations.

The planters of St. Domingue were exploited by French merchants who took advantage of their trade monopoly to fix arbitrary prices on the colonial products they bought and the manufactured goods they sold. French merchants could not supply the ever-growing demand for slaves. The planters of St. Domingue also wanted the right to purchase wheat directly from the United States. They complained of administrative incompetence and wanted to run the affairs of the colony themselves. Since the planters were heavily in debt to the merchants, their pull toward independence, especially after the American Revolution succeeded, was irresistible.[66] In the face of this sentiment favoring independence, the French Crown tried to stabilize its control over the colony by various means. Vigorous attempts to reform the slave system were undertaken and found legislative expression in the Ordonnances de Louis XVI. The Crown also toyed with the idea of protecting the colored elite from encroachments by the white planters: it hoped to rely upon the loyalty of the former as a safeguard against an independence movement among the latter.

The last tie which bound the white planters to France was their attachment, real or imagined, to the French nobility and their veneration of the king of France. The French Revolution snapped this final tie, and the Assembly of St. Marc, held on May 28, 1790, in effect declared independence in the name of the white planter class.[67] The ultimate result was the military victory of the slaves and independence of the colony under the control of the blacks.

The American Revolution resulted in the decline of the British West Indies and their fall from a preeminent place within the British Empire to a relatively insignificant status. The American Revolution cut off the main source of most of the capital goods needed on the estates; this led to an increase in the cost of production at a time when cheaper sugar, mainly from St. Domingue, was flooding the world market. An important market for the molasses exported from Jamaica was also lost, since the

[66] Gaston-Martin, *Histoire de l'esclavage dans les colonies françaises* (Paris: Presses Universitaires de France, 1948), pp. 172–77.
[67] *Ibid.*

British mainland colonies had bought most of this product before 1774.[68] British opposition to the African slave trade grew as her interest in her Caribbean colonies waned and her interest in the raw materials of Africa increased. The Amelioration Acts, beginning in 1780, attempted to stabilize the slave population and encourage its natural reproduction rather than rely upon the African slave trade.[69]

While the reform period presaged disaster in St. Domingue and reflected decline in the British West Indies, it had a very different meaning in Cuba. The attempt to create a slave code for the Spanish colonies was part of the Bourbon Reform Movement initiated under Charles III. Relaxation of mercantilist restrictions upon trade and imitation of the French model in law, administration, and economic theory were essential features of the Spanish Bourbon Reform Movement. By the 1780s, Spain began to explore the possibility that her Caribbean islands might become a significant source of wealth if slave plantation agriculture were encouraged. The slave codes of the Bourbon Reform period were intended to create a legal structure for a slave plantation system in the Spanish Caribbean. French slave law was used as the model. Several documents acknowledged conscious intent to copy French slave law. In 1781, the king of Spain attributed the backwardness of the Spanish Caribbean to its antiquated laws.

. . . the wisdom of the *Leyes de Indias* might have been good for the time in which they were established, and be today contrary to the circumstances in which we find ourselves. . . . the backwardness which we suffer should not be attributed to any other cause except to the Laws and Regulations with which we have been governed up to now.[70]

Cuba, Puerto Rico and Española, from their favorable situation, might have produced a large proportion of the products required by Europe. Yet Cuba was producing only 30,000 *cajas* of sugar and 40,000 *arrobas* of tobacco, while Puerto Rico and Española were almost entirely unproductive. Far less fertile and extensive foreign colonies produced and exported

[68] Orlando Patterson, *The Sociology of Slavery: An Analysis of the Origin, Development, and Structure of Negro Slave Society in Jamaica* (New York: Humanities Press, 1969), p. 27.

[69] *Ibid.*, pp. 76–78.

[70] Hubert H. S. Aimes, *A History of Slavery in Cuba, 1511 to 1868* (New York: G. P. Putnam's Sons, 1907), p. 40.

far more wealth than the vast possessions of Spain. The reason for this condition can be found in the laws.[71]

A Real Orden directed to the governor of Santo Domingo in 1783 by D. José Gálvez, Minister of the Indies, pointed out that the Spanish part of the island had not passed from the period of domestic slavery, while the French part was in the period of industrial slavery, and the Spanish should imitate the French. To achieve this aim, he ordered the formulation of "several ordinances for the economic, political, and moral regulation of the Negroes in this Island similar to the laws of the French which they call the Black Code."[72] The Reform Laws in the Spanish Caribbean were an attempt to create a legal structure for a slave plantation system which was in the process of being born. Sugar from St. Domingue was abruptly removed from the market with the outbreak of the Haitian Revolution, and Cuban sugar filled the vacuum. The disasters of the British and French Caribbean became the opportunities of Cuba.

All the laws of the reform period were concerned with promoting natural reproduction of the slave population. Encouragement of marriage and discouragement of illicit relations which tended to reduce fertility, sharp restrictions upon the work hours of female slaves, especially pregnant and nursing slaves, improvement of the nutrition of pregnant slaves, and care of the new-born slave infant were all concerns of the laws of the reform period. French law exempted the mother of six living children from all field work. Very similar provisions were contained in the Amelioration Acts for the British West Indies.[73]

Attempts were made to reduce mortality among slaves and prolong their working life by providing adequate care and protecting them from excessive labor and punishments. The Ordonnances de Louis XVI, dating from 1784–86, provided that a piece of land had to be supplied to each slave, male and female, as a garden plot, which was not to substitute for the master's responsibility to provide adequate food for his slave. The master was obliged to plant and maintain the necessary food crops for the abun-

[71] *Ibid.*

[72] Javier Malagon, "Un documento del siglo XVIII para la historia de la esclavitud en las Antillas," *Imago Mundo* 1, no. 9 (September, 1955):38–56.

[73] C.N.C., Cap. 26 and 146, Leyes 1, 2, and 3; C.N.E., Cap. 3, 5, and 7; *Loix*, Ordonnance de Louis XVI, December 3, 1784; Patterson, *Sociology of Slavery*, pp. 78, 111.

dant nourishment of the work force, and the crops raised by the slaves in their own gardens were not to be counted as part of the plantation food supply. Masters and overseers were to declare in the census the quantity of land they had planted in food crops, and the type of crops planted. Their reports were to be checked each year by the principal officer of the militia of the parish and reported to the governor or intendant. In case of false declaration or negligence, the matter was to be turned over to the royal prosecutor, who was empowered to levy an arbitrary fine without further procedure. As a safeguard against corruption of the inspectors, the governor-general himself, or his representative, was to visit plantations without notice to verify the truth of the declarations and certifications. Militia officers making inaccurate certifications were to be relieved of their posts and were to be subject to imprisonment or being broken to the ranks, and masters and overseers attempting to evade these provisions were to be subject to prosecution by the authorities. A minimum yearly clothing allotment was mandatory, and the masters were required to set up a clean, well-ventilated infirmary furnished with cots, linens, and blankets. Sick slaves were not to be allowed to sleep on the ground. A police force directly responsible to the intendant and the governor-general was created to inspect the estates and gather information about compliance with these laws.[74]

The Ordonnances de Louis XVI attempted to prevent excessive labor. Work on Sundays and holidays, night work, and work between noon and 2 p.m. were outlawed, except during the grinding season, when it could be carried on until 8 p.m. only. The Marechausée was to inspect the plantations and report at once any work going on during forbidden hours to the governor-general or intendant or to their representatives.[75]

Concern over protecting the slave from abuse by the master was also revived. Any owner, agent, or manager believed to have given more than fifty lashes to his slaves, or to have had them beaten with sticks, was to be punished by a 2,000-livres fine for the first offense, and declared incapable of owning slaves and returned to France for the second offense.

Aside from the above penalties, they shall be noted as infamous when they have had their slaves mutilated, and will incur the death penalty when they

---

[74] *Loix*, Ordonnances du Roi concernant les Procureurs et Economes-Gérans des Habitations situées aux Isles sous le Vent, December 3, 1784.

[75] *Loix*, Ordonnance du Roi, December 3, 1784, Titulo 11, Article 1.

have them killed under their private authority, for any cause whatsoever. His Majesty wills that they be, in this case, pursued diligently as murderers by his prosecutors, and orders the Governor-General and the Intendant to pay strict attention to this matter.[76]

Absentee ownership was widespread in late eighteenth-century St. Domingue, and during the reform period, the metropolis tried to control the practices of overseers and managers acting for absentee owners. Authorities in France advised: "It is necessary to severely repress the insolence of overseers, workers, and other employees under contract who dare carry out excesses against the proprietors."[77] One overseer was made civilly responsible for the loss of a cabaret, four mules, and two slaves which he was using for his own benefit without the consent of his employer.[78]

There was evidence of serious conflict between the overseer class and the colonial authorities. An order banished an overseer from the colony and fined him for inciting the slaves under his command to revolt against two government officials and cavalry officers who escorted them; the slaves, throwing stones and hoes, had pursued the officials. The Order was printed and displayed in public places.[79] Resistance to enforcement of the Ordonnances de Louis XVI was stiff, and the King complained that the managers

sought to persuade all those who make up the numerous class of agents of the plantations in the colony that their honor is at stake, and their status degraded. . . . They have alarmed them with fears about insubordination and desertion of slaves, and finally, some of them have threatened to abandon their posts and place the property in the hands of the Curator of Vacant Estates.

The King maintained that resistance to the Ordonnances arose "largely from the personal discontents of those among them whose vicious administration rendered this regulation necessary, so that they can perpetuate the abuses which they have interest to maintain." The king reiterated the practical nature of these reforms which "can best contribute to maintaining good order and conserve the slave work force in the interests of the masters

---

[76] Cited in Gisler, *L'Esclavage aux antilles françaises*, pp. 46, 47.

[77] *Loix*, Lettre du Ministre à M. le Marquis de Vaudreuil, nommé Gouverneur-Général, touchant la subordination des econ21omes, ouvriers et autres Gens a gages envers les Habitants, September 8, 1780.

[78] *Loix*, Arrêt du Conseil du Cap, July 11, 1781.

[79] *Loix*, Arrêt du Conseil du Port-au-Prince, July 11, 1785

and the security of their property." In response to resistance against enforcement of these reforms, an even stronger version was promulgated, revoking all previous laws which might conflict with the reform measures, and the new law was ordered to be read, published, and posted wherever necessary, and scrupulously complied with.[80]

This struggle demonstrates that there was little inclination on the part of the French Crown to abdicate its role as protector of the long-range interests of the slave system of St. Domingue, in spite of vigorous opposition from self-interested sectors of society. This determined attitude of the French Crown contrasts sharply with the impotent response of the Spanish Crown when faced with planter opposition to protective provisions of the Código Negro Español.

Spanish Slave Codes of the Reform Period

Two slave codes emerged from the Spanish reform efforts. The first code, the Código Negro Carolino (also referred to as the 1785 code) is more interesting insofar as it is a complete slave code written in the style of French law, explaining the policy considerations behind the measures formulated. The 1785 code was written for Santo Domingo, and although Spain lost that colony in 1795, and the code was in effect for only a decade, it reveals the policies and legal thought of the times. It is long, detailed, and unusually concrete for Spanish law. The purposes of the code were explained in its preamble. It was intended to overcome the decadence of the island by promoting plantation agriculture and thus "provide abundantly to the metropolis the products of its soil, facilitating the export of its crops and manufactures to reciprocally increase commerce and navigation." Large numbers of slaves were to be imported directly from Africa, and the slave and free Negro population was to be forced into agricultural labor. Emancipation was severely restricted.[81] A rigid caste system based upon race and a system of rewards and punishments intended to ensure the perfect subordination of the Negro population to "the magistrates, to their masters, and to white persons," were to be established.

The code was concerned with conversion to Catholicism and the par-

[80] *Loix*, Ordonnance du Roi, December 23, 1785.
[81] See Chapter 6 below.

ticipation of the slaves in the rituals of the Church. It outlawed pagan practices and music at funerals, and any assembly of slaves not under the supervision of whites. It was concerned with keeping the plantation slaves isolated and not allowing them to assemble with slaves from other plantations. Ecclesiastics were to visit the plantations so that estate slaves would not come into town and mix with free Negroes.

The master was to provide a garden plot or *conuco* to be cultivated by the slave for his own benefit. The *conuco* was not to substitute for providing food for slaves. In theory, the slave's right to personal property (*peculio*) was recognized in a very limited way. It was held at the discretion of the master, and could be seized by him in whole or in part if the slave misbehaved. In fact, the slave had no real property rights. "The slaves have no personality nor civil concept to acquire the very least right of possession or property which is not for the benefit of and at the mercy of their masters." It is clear that the *peculio* operated as a social myth promoting loyalty, justifying slavery, and promising some vague hope of emancipation for the plantation slave.

The other code which emerged from the Spanish Bourbon Reform period was the Código Negro Español (also referred to as the 1789 code). As its title (*Instrucción sobre la educación, trato y ocupación de los esclavos*) implies, it dealt almost exclusively with the protective aspects of slave law, and it did not pretend to be a complete code. Its Preface stated: ". . . in the interim that the general code is being formulated for the dominions of the Indies, the laws corresponding to this important matter are established and promulgated, and for now all owners and possessors of slaves in these dominions should punctually observe the following instructions." The 1789 code, dealing with limited aspects of slave law and written in the style of Spanish law, does not discuss the policy considerations behind the measures formulated. It was written for the entire Spanish Empire, but it was never promulgated in the Caribbean area where there was a substantial slave population—that is, in Santo Domingo, Cuba, Venezuela, and Louisiana which then belonged to Spain. Its provisions were in most respects similar to French law. In some respects—for example, failing to prohibit the separation of a mother and her child, if he was a minor, through sale or seizure—it was less protective than French law. In other respects—for example, providing criminal penalties for the abuse of slaves by persons other than their masters or overseers [82]—it was more protective.

Both Spanish Bourbon Reform codes provided that the master had to feed and clothe the slave. The 1785 code made suggestions about the amount of food and clothing which should be provided, but no fixed amount was made mandatory. The 1789 code provided that local officials were to establish the amounts. The 1785 code provided that the master could inflict punishment upon the slave "as long as it was not mutilation of a member, or did not endanger or cause the slave to lose his life, or subject him to interrogation under torture, in which case the master would be proceeded against in accordance with the gravity and atrocity of his crime" (a translation of the Code Noir). Prison, chains, stocks, irons, and other instruments used in the colonies were permitted by law. Flogging (*azotes de cujes o látigo*) "with just cause, moderation and opportunity not to exasperate them" was also allowed. The 1789 code limited the number of lashes to twenty-five, the number stipulated by the Code Noir, and allowed prison, chains, irons, and stocks, but the slave could not be placed in the stocks by the head. Flogging could be done only with a soft instrument which would not cause grave contusions or the flowing of blood, and only masters or overseers could impose these penalties. More severe penalties were to be imposed by law, "observing in all ways that which the laws dispose in cases of delinquents who are free" (a translation of the Code Noir). Violators were subject to fine, criminal proceedings could be started against the owner or overseer, and a penalty could be imposed corresponding to the crime committed, as it was when the injured party was free. If he was in condition to work, the injured slave could be confiscated, compensating the master for his price, and if disabled, he could be pensioned for life by the master.

The 1789 code required masters to maintain a list of their slaves and report the death or disappearance of a slave within three days. All slaves were to be accounted for annually "in order to avoid all suspicion of having violent death inflicted upon them." Visiting ecclesiastics were to report any neglect or abuse to the *procurador síndico* for investigation. A reputable person was to visit the estates three times a year, and officials

[82] C.N.E., Cap. 11.

were to be held accountable for their role as protectors of slaves. There was little in the 1789 code which was not contained in French slave law of much earlier times. It was not a *uniquely protective code compared with French and British slave law of the reform period.*

Another Spanish Bourbon Reform law which has often been cited as a humanitarian measure was the abandonment by Spanish customs officials of the practice of branding Negro slaves. The text of the law explained that branding had been used to distinguish legally imported slaves from contraband slaves; they now had other means to do so, and the brands were to be taken away from the officials of the Cajas Reales. The law did not outlaw branding by the master. It appears to be simply a prelude to declaring free trade in slaves.[83]

The Myth of Protective Spanish Slave Law

The effort to formulate and promulgate a slave code for the Spanish Caribbean during the Bourbon Reform period collapsed. This fact, however, has not discouraged scholars publishing in English from relying heavily upon the text of the unpromulgated Código Negro Español to prove that slavery in the Spanish Caribbean was a mild institution. This process began long ago, in 1910, when Harry H. Johnson published *The Negro in the New World.* Fernando Ortiz commented upon Johnson's error as follows, "In this book of *precipitous* erudition, this Real Cédula is given as if it were in force, and following from this error, not a few comments are made."[84] Ortiz' remark, published in 1916, has not discouraged contemporary comparative historians from continuing to comment ecstatically about the benevolent paternalism of this unpromulgated code.[85]

Since transcendental theories, based upon the assumption that Latin American slavery was mild, are being constructed by scholars outside the field of Latin American history, it might be a contribution to critical scholar-

---

[83] *DHFS*, Real Orden, November 4, 1784, vol. 3, pp. 543–44.

[84] Ortiz, *Los negros esclavos*, p. 364.

[85] The latest example is Klein, *Slavery in the Americas*, pp. 78–85, where five pages are devoted to the details of the Código Negro Español and one page to dubious generalities about the slave law of nineteenth-century Cuba. "Although the law might be more or less enforced in given periods, we can nevertheless assume that by the nineteenth century the attitudes universally expressed in the vast body of canonical and civil law of Spain and Cuba had come to be accepted as legitimate and morally operative by the majority of Cuban whites."

ship to review in detail the history of the non-promulgation of the Código Negro Español. José Antonio Saco explained:

When the Real Cédula of May 31, 1789 was sent out, the planters around Havana met on January 20, 1790, and together with those of Santo Domingo, Caracas, and New Orleans . . . petitioned the government through their *ayuntamientos* not to publish the Code for fear that the slaves, misinterpreting its meaning, could rise in insurrection. Actually, the captains-general did not publish it; and the Council of the Indies, after consulting Francisco de Saavedra, Ignacio de Urriza, and other persons acquainted with American affairs who all recommended the suspension of the Code, agreed to the formation in each provincial capital of a *junta* composed of the principal landowners, the bishop, and the captain-general to make proposals for the regulation of slavery.[86]

The report to the Consejo de las Indias by Juan Ignacio de Urriza stated:

What evidently happened is that many difficulties came up at the time of putting this law into practice, as experience has already begun to show. The colonists, doubtful of reaping the fruits of their industry, repeated their clamours with greater vehemence. The magistrates became perplexed again, and uncertainties and fears arose from the details of the Cédula that arbitrariness and passion might enter and that the justices and subalterns, who have always demonstrated in the Indies more propensity to abuse their authority against the citizens than the masters their power over their Negroes, might find an open door through which to spy on the hacendados.

Urriza proposed a junta of officials, ecclesiastics, two *hacendados*, and two *comerciantes* in each parish to promulgate local ordinances.[87]

Further progress of the matter can be followed in a Consulta del Consejo de la Indias dating from 1794.

It is proposed that the effects of the Real Cédula be suspended and that, without the necessity to revoke it, nor to carry out the *juntas* that have been proposed, it shall suffice for now that we secretly charge the tribunals and *jefes* of America that, without publishing it, nor doing anything else, that they try in particular cases and occurrences which present themselves to

---

[86] Quoted in Ortiz, *Los negros esclavos*, p. 364.

[87] Informe de Juan Ignacio de Urriza, Francisco de Saavedra, Don Antonio Ventura de Tranaco to the Consejo de las Indias, January 3, 1792, in José Antonio Saco, *Historia de la esclavitud de la raza africana en el Nuevo Mundo y en especial en los países Américo-Hispanos*, 4 vols. (Havana: Cultural S.A., 1938), Appendix, 3:247–78.

act in conformity with the spirit of its articles, keeping firmly in view that the laws and other dispositions given for the good treatment and Christian education of the Negroes be observed.

His Majesty resolved to suspend further action on the code until after the war.[88] A Real Cédula dating from 1804 contented itself with exhorting that slaves be treated humanely, and suggested that female slaves be introduced on estates where there were only males until all desiring marriage were married, but these suggestions were not to be published for fear the slaves might hear about them. After this date, *sindicos municipales* were activated in urban areas, but they never operated in the countryside where "the slave regime on the plantations continued unchecked [*irrefrenado*]."[89] An official guide for the protectors of slaves issued by the Real Audiencia of Cuba commented about the regulation of work hours contained in the 1789 code, "But this is not observed, and neither the magistrates regulate the time of labour, nor do the slaves cease to serve their masters at all hours."[90] When a proposal was made in 1847 to publish those chapters of the 1789 code dealing with religious education, the intendant remarked, "We should not try to restore the effect of any of the articles of the Real Cédula of May 31, 1789, which created such alarm among the proprietors of the island, and whose dispositions remain and shall remain in suspension."[91] Thus, efforts made during the Bourbon Reform period to legislate concrete forms of protection for slaves dissolved back into the humanitarian phrasemongering typical of Spanish law of earlier times.[92]

---

[88] *DHFS*, Consulta del Consejo de las Indias, March 17, 1794, vol. 3, pp. 726–32.

[89] Ortiz, *Los negros esclavos*, p. 366.

[90] Richard R. Madden, *The Island of Cuba* (London, 1853), p. 132.

[91] A.H.N. Ultramar, Legajo 4655, No. 816, Testimonios del expediente formado para averiguar las causes que influyen en el frecuente suicidio de los esclavos, Informe del Conde de Villanueva, Havana, June 30, 1847.

[92] Ferrer de Couto, a defender of the Cuban slave regime, interpreted these decisions as follows: "It is true that the said *Ordenanzas* suffered some contradiction when hardly promulgated, by virtue of the petition to His Majesty by some proprietors and industrialists of the Islands of Cuba and Santo Domingo and from Caracas on the continent, from which resulted very luminous and authoritative reports by great experts; and the opinion was for the suspension of some articles, confirming all those that referred to the good treatment and the humane charity with which the Negroes should be treated in all the Spanish possessions." Don José Ferrer de Couto, *Los negros en sus diversos estados y condiciones; tales como son, como se supone que son, y como deben ser*, 2d ed. (New York: Hallet Press, 1864), p. 64.

SLAVE LAW OF NINETEENTH-CENTURY CUBA

Although Cuba had developed a flourishing slave plantation system by the early nineteenth century, it was not until 1842 that a new effort was made to provide concrete legal protection to Cuban slaves. During the four and a half centuries of the history of Cuba, the sovereign will of the master knew no limits except those dictated by his "doubtful piety and sure interest."[93] The 1842 code made specific minimum requirements for food and clothing, and set limitations upon punishment similar to those contained in the 1789 code. Two years after the 1842 code had been promulgated, its protective aspects were nullified as a reaction to the Conspiracy of the Ladder. Two Providencias de Policía reestablished the prudent judgment of the masters. These laws provided that the masters,

> . . . using in all its fullness the sovereign authority [*autoridad domínica*] over their serfs which the laws concede to them as the only means of maintaining them in subordination, . . . to any of said employees that they give the food, clothing, and care during their illness which their prudent judgment [*prudente arbitrio*] estimes convenient, and that they punish said serfs when they are delinquent with prison or lashes in the number and for the time that the one in charge considers in conformity with the instructions which in each case he may have received from the master . . . [inclining] more toward moderation than toward excess.[94]

Attempts to regulate work hours also deteriorated. The 1789 code limited the working day from sunrise to sunset, with two hours off during the day. The 1842 code provided for a ten-hour work day, except during the grinding season, when it was increased to sixteen hours. The law of 1880, abolishing slavery and establishing a system whereby the slaves were called *patrocinados*, required that they normally be given seven hours for sleep, two hours of free time each day, but "on the country estates one can require, during the *zafra* (grinding season), the necessary work hours, according to custom."[95]

Corporal punishment remained legal until late in the nineteenth century. In 1870, flogging was outlawed, but stocks, irons, and private jails

---

[93] Ortiz, *Los negros esclavos*, p. 370.

[94] Ferrer de Couto, *Los negros en sus estados*, pp. 80–83; see also Ortiz, *Los negros esclavos*, p. 377.

[95] *Código penal vigente en las islas de Cuba y Puerto Rico* (Madrid: Pedro Nuñez, 1886), p. 233; Ley y Reglamento de Abolición de la esclavitud, Cap. 2, Article 28.

were still permitted. It was not until 1880 that a scale of offenses and their punishments was legislated.[96] Finally, in 1883, three years after the abolitionist law, the Spanish Crown, continuing its long tradition of congratulating itself upon its extraordinary humanitarianism, promulgated the following decree in honor of the Royal birthday, "No better occasion could offer itself to make patent the magnanimous sentiments of humanity and progress which exalts the character of Your Majesty," and stocks and irons were at last outlawed in Cuba.[97] Although the *patronato* was ended in 1886, the former slaves still constituted a special class called *libertos* and were subject to forced labor and special vigilance by the police. Full freedom was not legalized until 1890.[98]

To explain the contrast between the myth of protective Spanish slave law and the reality, one must deal with the history of history, and the myth-making role which history often plays in human affairs. The myth of protective Spanish slave law and the mildness of the Spanish slave system originated in the ideological defense of the slave system of nineteenth-century Cuba. Rafael María de Labra, writing years after slavery had been abolished, commented upon the great success of propaganda favoring the slave interests. "One has to admire the nerve by which they propagated the belief that the slaves of the Antilles lived happily and contented. . . . No one mentioned dungeons, stocks and irons, nor the awful mortality rate among slaves."[99] The myth was bolstered by Ferrer De Couto's history, published in 1864 defending Cuban slavery and the African slave trade, in which the writer claimed that the Spanish slave law had always been very protective, and the 1789 code was simply a codification of existing law into a uniform body of law.[100] He described the 1789 code as a

protective and highly humanitarian code, such as no other nation has ever made for its most favored proletarians, from which we infer that the treatment and legislation observed with the Negroes since their importation into the Spanish colonies does not correspond to the quality of slaves, not

[96] Ortiz, *Los negros esclavos*, pp. 267–68.
[97] *Código penal Cuba y Puerto Rico*, Real decreto suprimiendo los castigos del cepo y el grillete en la isla de Cuba, pp. 267–68.
[98] Ortiz, *Los negros esclavos*, p. 389.
[99] Rafael María de Labra y Cadrana, *La reforma política de Ultramar, 1868–1900* (Madrid: Alfredo Alonso, 1902), p. 22, cited in Arthur F. Corwin, *Spain and the Abolition of Slavery in Cuba, 1817–1886* (Austin and London: University of Texas Press, 1967), p. 312.
[100] Ferrer de Couto, *Los negros en sus estados*, pp. 52–53.

at all [*ni mucho menos*]; rather they seem to be more like free colonists subject to a reasonable contract; and more so since the door was even opened to their freedom by means of application and the benefit of individual ability, for all the Negroes who wished to receive it.[101]

The Código Negro Español did indeed claim in its preamble that it was a codification of existing slave law in force in the Spanish colonies. The claim was false. It was copied largely from the French Code Noir of 1685, and from the Ordonnances de Louis XVI. A search of Spanish slave law predating the 1789 code reveals a conspicuous absence of concrete protective measures.[102]

THE IMPACT OF CORRUPTION IN PUBLIC OFFICE

There were, moreover, special obstacles to enforcement of any law in nineteenth-century Cuba. Dr. Madden, who granted the "excellence of the Spanish civil law," raised serious questions about whether the law could be enforced against the planter. As the

friend of the authorities of his district, they dare not disoblige him, and if they dared, they are at last to be gained over by a bride, or got rid of by a remonstrance to the governor, and a suitable present to the assessor of the governor, who is one of the great law officers of the Crown. . . . The iniquity of Spanish tribunals, the corruption of Spanish judges, and the incomparable villainy of Spanish lawyers is proverbial in all the colonies of Spain. Justice is bought and sold in Cuba with as much scandalous publicity as the Bozal slaves are bought and sold in the barracoons.[103]

Madden concluded that a show was made of surrounding the compulsions of slavery with "humane arrangements, duly detailed in the royal cédulas, and set forth in legal books, *with all the solemn mockery of Spanish law*" [His italics].[104] Dr. Wurdemann has left us a very unflattering picture of the Capitanes de Partida, who

---

[101] *Ibid.*, pp. 60–61.

[102] Frank Tannenbaum accepted this false claim. See *Slave and Citizen: The Negro in the Americas* (New York: Alfred A. Knopf, 1946), p. 53. I was unable to verify the references to protective Spanish slave law prior to 1789 contained in Elsa V. Goveia, "The West Indian Slave Laws of the Eighteenth Century," *Revista de ciencias sociales* 4 (March, 1960):75–105. For a comparison of slave law of the British, French, and Spanish colonies prior to the Bourbon Reform period, see Petit, *Gouvernement des esclaves*, 2 vols. (Paris: Knapen, 1777).

[103] Madden, *Island of Cuba*, pp. 122–24.

[104] *Ibid.*, pp. 119–24.

like so many vultures . . . prey upon the unprotected within their jurisdiction. Nor are the rich without the pale of their power, and those who have not influence with the heads of the island government are sometimes largely fleeced by them on most frivolous pretexts. [He describes one of them.] While riding through the country with sword and pistols, his slouched hat, goatee that had crawled up on his shoulders, and pantaloons struggling to escape from their straps, his face unshaven, and his whole person covered with dust, he might readily have been taken for a prowling thief.[105]

This chapter does not deal with the question of whether or not the slave was defined as a chattel. There is much documentation on this aspect of slave law in St. Domingue which makes it abundantly clear that it was unimportant to the slave whether he was considered a chattel, a semi-chattel, or real estate, and these definitions are unrelated to the question of whether or not the slave had a legal personality. They relate to circumstances under which the slave could be seized for debt, and whether or not the slaves of an estate could be divided among heirs. French law, while defining the slave as a chattel, afforded great protection against seizure for debt, since field slaves could not be so seized apart from the land, and it was almost impossible to execute a judgment in St. Domingue by seizing an estate. In fact, much of the prosperity of St. Domingue was based upon the extraordinary protection enjoyed by the planters against any form of seizure for debt. The planters of the British West Indies were at a severe disadvantage in this regard. In contrast, while slaves in the British West Indies could not be divided among heirs, those of the French islands could be so divided. In any case, whether the slave was defined as chattel or real estate, he could be freely sold apart from the land at will by the master.[106]

It should be unnecessary to insist upon the obvious in any discussion of the value of law as a historical source. The text of law alone proves little except, at times, the intentions of its formulators. The determination and ability of the state to enforce the law and the role which corruption in public office plays in subverting it are factors which cannot be ignored. The weaving of theories based largely upon the text of an unpromulgated law tells us much more about the alienation from reality of much of the

---

[105] J. G. F. Wurdemann, *Notes on Cuba* (Boston: James Monroe and Co., 1844), pp. 129–30.

[106] For an interesting discussion of the slave as chattel, see David Brian Davis, *The Problem of Slavery in Western Culture* (Ithaca: Cornell University Press, 1966), pp. 244–53.

historical profession than it tells us about the slave system in the Spanish Caribbean.

Slave societies, especially sugar colonies in a prosperous condition, were highly combustible. The get-rich-quick mentality of the planters and their managers generated conditions which were highly destructive to the slave population and undermined the stability of the colony. Revenues from these colonies, both direct and indirect, were vast, and the metropolis had a great deal at stake as it sought to prevent interest groups within the colonies from killing the goose that laid the golden eggs. Generally, the metropolis embraced a broader, more long-range point of view than did the planter class. The texts of slave laws formulated by the metropolis were likely to be reasonably concerned with preventing abuses which might transcend limits conducive to the survival of the colony.

While protective aspects of French slave law were impressive, it would be naive to conclude, as Antoine Gisler did, that it represents "a permanent effort in view of safeguarding to this order, to this society, in brief, to slavery, a humane character, respectful of the dignity and the essential rights of the slave."[107] The motivations of slave law were eminently practical. The contrast between French and Spanish slave law lay not in various degrees of humanitarianism between the two colonizing powers. It was in the interests of both powers to curb abuses within the slave system. Spanish slave law, at least its protective aspects, was weak before the late eighteenth century because there was no slave plantation society in the Spanish colonies requiring extensive regulation. It was weak after the late eighteenth century because Spain was unable to impose her will upon the Cuban planters. The situation in nineteenth-century Cuba was further complicated by the fact that colonial officials, and some individuals in the highest ranks of the Spanish state, had a vested interest in the continuation of the African slave trade once it became illegal. The slave system in the Cuban countryside was uncontrolled. The Cuban authorities abdicated their role as regulator of the system, relying instead upon a large standing army organized into mobile units to cut down the slaves as they revolted. Costly as this kind of rule was to the planters, overkill became the major method of controlling the slaves in nineteenth-century Cuba.

[107] Gisler, *L'Esclavage aux antilles françaises*, p. 98.

VI

EMANCIPATION AND THE
STATUS OF THE FREE

THE PROBLEM OF WHETHER a particular slave system encouraged or discouraged emancipation and the subject of the status enjoyed by people of African descent once they were free have often been discussed by comparative historians. Social control, however, has been neglected; the slave systems have been viewed either as being static or as being developmental (that is, as time progressed, they became more humanitarian). Fragmentary and sometimes distorted evidence has often been assembled to prove or disprove a preconceived theory. Here, as elsewhere, an intelligent discussion demands that we establish the pattern of rise and decline of the particular slave plantation system, the impact of one system upon another, and the very real problems of social control motivating policies in these matters.

It is very clear from the evidence relating to formulation of policy that preexisting racial attitudes were relatively insignificant. Pressures within and upon these societies were intense, and policies were based not on racial attitudes but on fundamental military, economic, social, and political concerns. These concerns often conflicted with one another and their changing order of priority was reflected in the changes in policy toward emancipation and the status of the free.

In St. Domingue, where the metropolis asserted its right to determine policy in its own interests, little sentimentality crept into policy discussions.

"The property rights of the masters have never been the reason for tolerating slavery in the colonies," wrote Emilien Petit. "The establishment of the lands was, and is, the sole aim, in the interest of commerce."[1] Petit maintained that the French government should encourage or restrict emancipation in the interests of the stability of the colony, regardless of the desires of the masters. His strategy was a middle course: restrict emancipation to keep enough working hands, but do not restrict it so much that it produces a dangerous state of despair among the slaves, because "only the hope for liberty can sustain or animate the fidelity of the slaves in a state of degradation and poverty, and attach them to their masters, or to white blood, which amounts to the same thing."[2]

The Predominance of Military Considerations during the Pre-plantation Period

We have seen that obtaining white colonists during the early years of colonization was a difficult problem in both the Spanish and French Caribbean. Before the rise of the slave plantation systems, there were few attractions for colonists. At the same time, rivalry over control of the islands was intense, not for economic reasons, but because the British and French islands were viewed as bridgeheads to the gold- and silver-producing Spanish mainland colonies. Once the Spanish territorial monopoly of the Caribbean was breached, the principle of effective occupation determined which power would control which islands. Emancipation was encouraged, and freedmen enjoyed relatively high status because the colonizers needed to count as many heads as possible, and because the free colored population, and even, at times, the slaves, were effectively used for military purposes.

Because of the availability of white settlers, the military role of the slaves and the free colored population was apparently less prominent in the British colonies, which quickly became colonies of economic exploitation; the free colored population, however, was the major military force in the Spanish and French Caribbean. Africans were the principal military and police force throughout the history of St. Domingue, even after the

---

[1] Emilien Petit, *Traité sur le gouvernement des esclaves*, 2 vols. (Paris: Knapen, 1777), 2:68.
[2] *Ibid.*, vol. 2, p. 69.

rise of the slave plantation system, and this situation was a major factor in the success of the Haitian Revolution. In Cuba, however, the military role of the free colored population declined with the emergence of the slave plantation system, and the colored militia was superseded by a large standing army of Spanish troops during the nineteenth century.

There was a long history of using Africans for military purposes. The process began on the slave trade ships. Captain Hugh Crow selected likely young blacks from his cargo, armed them, and taught them to fire at a bottle hung from the yardarm. Every man who hit the target was given a cap and a drink of grog. If the vessel was attacked, Crow expected the slaves to help defend it, and he reported that they never disappointed him.[3] Billy Boates armed his slaves and fought off French pirates near the Leeward Islands in 1758. Several other captains found that the Africans fought well during the course of the voyage.[4]

Slaves were also used for military purposes in the Portuguese colonies. During the civil war between the Paulistas and the Emboabas of Brazil over control of the mines, the latter had African slaves fighting on their side, and the former had Indians.[5] French reliance upon the military possibilities of the Africans dated from the earliest years of their colonization of the Caribbean. Dutertre reported:

They are valiant and hardy in the face of danger, and during all the desperate encounters which our colonists of St. Christopher Island have had from time to time with the English, they have been no less redoubtable to this nation than their masters. M. d'Enambuc used them advantageously to repulse the British, and M. le Commandeur de Salles, seeing himself in this year 1666 with the choice between victory and death, used them to chase these irreconcilable enemies of our Nation from the Island. And they have done their duty, so well—setting fires everywhere while our Frenchmen were in battle,—that they have made no small contribution to the famous victory which France won over England.[6]

[3] Daniel Pratt Mannix, in collaboration with Malcolm Cowley, *Black Cargoes: History of the Atlantic Slave Trade* (New York: Viking Press, 1962), p. 137.

[4] *Ibid.*, pp. 131, 132.

[5] C. R. Boxer, *The Golden Age of Brazil* (Berkeley and Los Angeles: University of California Press, 1962), pp. 61–83.

[6] Jean-Baptiste Dutertre, *Histoire générale des antilles habitées par les françois*, 4 vols. (Paris: 1667–71), 2:499.

Throughout the history of St. Domingue, free blacks, mulattoes, and slaves were mobilized to pursue fugitive slaves, to defend the border with Spain, and to participate in the frequent colonial wars in the Caribbean. In 1695, slaves were offered 10 ecus for each enemy head, 10 ecus for each deserter returned to an officer, and freedom for taking an enemy officer or an enemy flag or for saving the life of a subject of the king.[7] Trusted plantation slaves were mobilized again in 1709, "experience having proved that one can make very good use of the Nègres des Habitans."[8] A company composed of whites and mulattoes was organized to guard the Spanish border. In default of whites, free blacks could also be received into the company.[9] Free blacks were conscripted into military service in 1724 and organized into the Compagnie de Nègres-Libres, which was divided into three to four squadrons, each under an officer. The main duty of this company was to pursue fugitive slaves.[10] The Maréchausée, a militarized police force, was reorganized in 1733, and archers were chosen from among free blacks and mulattoes.[11] In 1740, the French king, complaining that the white colonists were too "soft" even in defense of "their own property," recommended an increase in emancipations to augment the military strength of the colony, because the free blacks had always been regarded as "the principal force of the colony."[12]

As the slave plantation system developed, however, internal security problems became more severe and exerted pressure against using Africans for military purposes. Following the Mackandal Conspiracy, exposed in 1758, masters expressed fears that the arming and military training of slaves would undermine discipline, and they insisted upon training and leading their own slaves. It was decided that in no case could slaves form a separate body of troops.[13] But the free colored population continued to

[7] Loix, Arrêt du Conseil de Guerre pour la défense de la Colonie en cas d'attaque, February 17, 1695.
[8] Loix, Ordonnance des Administrateurs touchant les Nègres à armer en temps de guerre, September 9, 1709.
[9] Loix, Ordonnance des Administrateurs, March 27, 1721.
[10] Loix, Règlement fait par le Gouverneur du Cap pour la Compagnie des Nègres-Libres de la Dépendance de la même ville, April 29, 1724.
[11] Loix, Ordonnance des Administrateurs, January 20, 1733.
[12] Loix, Lettre du Ministre à M. de Larnage sur les Milices, June 3, 1740.
[13] Loix, Ordonnance des Administrateurs, March 12, 1759.

be relied upon heavily for defense, and in 1762, the Compagnie de Chasseurs de Gens de Couleur, consisting of volunteer free blacks and mulattoes, was organized for the duration of the war only.[14] This body of troops was still in existence in 1768, when the commanders were ordered to use it for the pursuit of fugitive slaves and deserters and for policing the neighborhoods.[15]

In 1779, the king, expressing full confidence in the attachment and fidelity of his free colored subjects, formed the Corps de Chasseurs Volontaires de Gens de Couleur de St. Domingue, consisting of 600 volunteers.[16] A general conscription of free men of color was ordered in 1780. All blacks, mulattoes, and free colored men between fifteen and sixteen years of age were ordered to serve one year in the Compagnies de Chasseurs-Royaux of their department. No ratification of emancipation could be made until the subject had served one year in the said companies.[17] Upon the departure of most of the garrison on a major expedition, the commander of the Batallion of Limonade was ordered to call up the colored militia to help garrison the island.[18] Two captains of the Compagnie de Nègres-Libres, both age ninety-six, were given lifetime (*sic*) pensions from the government. "The said Etienne Auba," said the order, "has always given to his numerous family, as well as to the people of his color, the best example of respect, of obedience, and of submission to the government as well as to the whites."[19]

Moreau de St.-Méry boasted of what an excellent soldier the mulatto was, proving his ability in the Maréchaussée, in the Chasseurs formed by M. de Belzince in 1762, and in the Chasseurs-Royaux who marched on Savannah, Georgia in 1779. It was the mulattoes, St.-Méry wrote, who usually pursued fugitive slaves. He pointed out that military life has its attractions for the idle and pleasure-loving, and the mulatto is content with little, living off roots and tropical fruits. He needs almost no clothes,

---

[14] *Loix*, Ordonnance du Gouverneur-Général, April 29, 1762.

[15] *Loix*, Ordonnance du Roi, April 1, 1768.

[16] *Loix*, Ordonnance du Gouverneur-Général, March 12, 1779.

[17] *Loix*, Ordonnance du Commandent en Chef par interim, May 26, 1780.

[18] *Loix*, Lettre du Gouverneur-Général au Commandant du Bataillon de Limonade, April 15, 1782.

[19] *Loix*, Ordonnances des administrateurs, July 8, 1776 and August 11, 1779.

can stand the sun, and can climb mountains with agility, But he should not be confined to the barracks at night because "night belongs to pleasure." [20] It is, unfortunately, only too rare that poetic justice is meted out as it was in St. Domingue, where this cynical policy of degrading and exploiting a population to fulfill the military needs of the rulers so thoroughly backfired.

The Spanish colonial authorities took similar measures to "obtain some utility from and control over an ever more numerous population which insistently eluded the political ideal for the citizen of the epoch." In the early seventeenth century, *compañías de negros y mulatos libres* or armed bodies known as *compañías de pardos* (the latter term most often used in Cuba) were organized throughout the Spanish Empire. This practice intensified as the governmental structure of social control weakened and as Spanish authorities became increasingly incapable of maintaining a royal army adequate for the defense of the American colonies.[21] Because of the primarily strategic role which Cuba played during the seventeenth and eighteenth centuries, and the inadequacy of Spanish resources to defend the island, the numerous free colored population was allowed a reasonably decent status in order to promote loyalty to the metropolis, and was heavily relied upon for defense.[22] Once the move toward slave plantation agriculture gained momentum, however, military considerations came into conflict with economic necessities and concern about internal stability. By the late 1820s, 15,000 veteran Spanish troops were stationed in Cuba, and between 15,000 and 20,000 such troops remained in Cuba until the 1860s.[23] The *pardo* (mulatto) and *moreno* (black) militia companies and battalions played only a vestigial role, until they were formally dissolved in 1844.[24] When they were reestablished in 1854 in the face of annexationist threats from the United States, they were subordinated to the regular commands and placed under the jurisdiction of royal battalions. The danger of arm-

[20] M. L. E. Moreau de St.-Méry, *Description topographique, physique, civile, politique, et historique de la partie française de l'Isle Saint-Domingue*, 4 vols. (Philadelphia, 1797), 1:103, 104.

[21] Rolondo Mellafe, *La esclavitud en Hispanoamérica* (Buenos Aires: Eudeba Editorial Universitaria de Buenos Aires, 1964), pp. 84, 85.

[22] Herbert S. Klein, *Slavery in the Americas: A Comparative Study of Virginia and Cuba* (Chicago: University of Chicago Press, 1967), pp. 214–18.

[23] *Ibid.*, p. 219.

[24] *Ibid.*, p. 221.

ing and giving military training to a degraded sector of the population was also manifested in Cuba. "Many a colored officer trained by the Spanish would rise to a position of prominence in the rebel armies." [25]

POLICY TOWARD EMANCIPATION AND THE NEEDS OF PLANTATION AGRICULTURE

The colonizing powers initiated the slave system with few preconceptions about encouraging or discouraging emancipation. It eventually became evident that if no restrictions were placed upon emancipation, the free colored population would grow rapidly. During the pre-plantation periods in Cuba and St. Domingue, the existence of a large, free colored population was a military advantage. In both colonies, however, the development of a plantation system brought with it hostility toward the emancipation of slaves and vigorous attempts from the metropolis to severely limit the right of the master to free his slave at will, the obvious reason being that a slave plantation system required large numbers of slaves to work in agriculture. Freed slaves tended overwhelmingly to abandon agriculture and flock to the cities and towns; this created a serious control problem. Spanish policy on emancipation is clear from a document dating from 1788, when the metropolis was attempting to encourage plantation agriculture in Cuba. This document pointed out that the slaves were the working hands necessary to maintain an agricultural system and that when they were slaves, they could be obliged by direct means to work and cultivate the land, but that once they were freed, many of them abandoned themselves to "idleness and other vices," requiring the government to exercise vigilance over them. "It is advisable to keep in mind the political inconveniences which would follow from facilitating this benefit too much in the areas where slaves are indispensable for the cultivation of the land and for the exploitation of its fruits and productions." [26]

Francisco d'Arango y Parreño, arguing against the abolition of the African slave trade, pointed out that such a measure would "wipe out the black race where it is useful and favor its increase where it is pernicious." During the previous twenty years, the free colored population of Havana

---

[25] *Ibid.*, p. 222.
[26] *DHFS*, Consulta del Consejo de las Indias, vol. 3, pp. 631–35.

had increased by 171 percent, the slave population by 165 percent, and the white population by only 73 percent. "To consider taking violent measures to chase these, in general, corrupt people from the towns and transport them to the countryside would be to wish to accomplish the impossible, and would produce perhaps greater injustices and the most terrible disasters." The free colored were drawn away from agriculture "perhaps because of the little protection found by those who enter it without large amounts of capital and large means," and were attracted to the cities because of "the facilities which the large towns offer for their vices, or the preference they have for the mechanical arts."[27] Leopoldo O'Donnell, captain-general of Cuba, reported that freed slaves offered no advantage for the promotion of agriculture.[28] They were entirely incapable of labor on the sugar estates, the proof being that there was not one emancipated slave, even among those granted freedom on the sugar estates, who remained in the sugar country to earn his living.[29]

The tendency of the plantation slave to abandon the plantation wherever and whenever feasible was a widespread phenomenon. Following abolition of slavery in the larger Caribbean islands like Jamaica, where unoccupied land was available, freedmen developed subsistence agriculture and only occasionally offered themselves for hire to the labor market. Parliamentary Commissions reporting on the causes for the decline of the sugar industry following the abolition of slavery attributed the decline largely to the labor shortage.

Distress . . . has been so great in the larger colonies of Jamaica, British Guiana, and Trinidad that it has caused many estates, hitherto prosperous and productive, to be cultivated for the past two or three years at a loss, and others to be abandoned. . . . Cheapness of land [is] the main cause of the difficulty. . . . the laborers are enabled to live in comfort, and to acquire wealth without for the most part laboring on the estates of the planters for more than three or four days in the week, and from five to seven hours a day.

[27] *Recueil de diverses pièces et des discussions qui ont eu lieu aux Cortes Générales sur l'abolition de la Traite et de l'esclavage des Nègres* (Paris, 1814), p. 65.
[28] A.H.N. Ultramar, Legajo 3550, Expediente 16, No. 854, Raza Blanca y de Color, Carta de Capitan-Général O'Donnell al Sec. de Estado, November 10, 1847.
[29] *Ibid.*

It was reported in 1848 that of the 653 estates operating in Jamaica in 1832, 140 had been abandoned. In 138 estates still operating, production fell from 17,000 tons in 1832 to 11,400 tons. Laborers fell from 41,820 to 13,973, the balance of 27,847 having become squatters or independent farmers. An investigation into the failure of a sugar company organized in Jamaica in 1844 revealed that the blacks would work only about six to seven hours a day for three or four days a week, and even then, not very hard. They refused to work longer hours, even for high wages. They refused piece work, except at a very high rate. If it rained during crop time, they gathered their own crops and failed to show up for work on the estate.[30]

The Haitian Revolution led to the dissolution of the plantation system in St. Domingue and the emergence of subsistence agriculture. After the abolition of slavery in the coffee regions of Brazil, when the freedmen found that they could meet their minimum needs by working two or three days a week, they preferred to "buy leisure" rather than earn anything extra.[31] In contrast, on small islands like Antigua, where neither land for subsistence agriculture nor employment in towns was available, labor costs did not increase and the sugar industry did not decline after the abolition of slavery.[32] The experience of estate owners using contract laborers in mid-nineteenth-century Cuba was typical. Workers brought from the Canary Islands were subject to a military regime, and penalties ranging from imprisonment to death were imposed for deserting work. Miguel Estorch of the *ingenio* La Colonia attempted to operate with Catalonian contract workers without imposing a military regime upon them. The workers refused to work eighteen hours a day during the *zafra*, and deserted to less arduous and higher-paying jobs.[33]

[30] Noel Deerr, *The History of Sugar*, 2 vols. (London: Chapman and Hall, Ltd., 1950), 2:362–70.

[31] Celso Furtado, *The Economic Growth of Brazil: A Survey from Colonial to Modern Times*, trans. Ricardo W. De Aguiar and Eric O. Drysdale (Berkeley and Los Angeles: University of California Press, 1963), pp. 153–54.

[32] Deerr, *History of Sugar*, vol. 2, p. 368.

[33] Manuel Moreno Fraginals, *El ingenio: El complejo económico social cubano del azucar* (Havana: Comisión Nacional Cubana de la UNESCO, 1964), pp. 147–149. The contrast between Cuba and Puerto Rico is instructive. During the late 1840s, when the colonial authorities of Cuba were very concerned about increasing the slave population there, the capitain-general of Puerto Rico communicated to the

In colonies where an economic alternative to plantation labor existed, slavery or another form of forced labor, either direct or indirect, was necessary to maintain plantation agriculture. Since an adequate labor force on the estates was an essential concern of policy-makers encouraging plantation agriculture, restriction upon the right of the master to emancipate a slave at will consequently characterized societies evolving in this direction.

THE EVOLUTION OF FRENCH POLICY TOWARD EMANCIPATION

French policy evolved from placing no restrictions whatsoever upon emancipation to increasing limitations intended to make it very difficult for the master to free his slave. During the strategic period of colonization, the Code Noir allowed masters who were twenty years old or older to emancipate their slaves without the consent of their parents. This right was revoked in 1721, for the stated reason that young masters were abusing this right and thereby ruining their estates; this was resulting in a "considerable prejudice to our colonies, the principal utility of which depends upon the labor of the Negroes who give value to the lands." [34] By the early eighteenth century, a government permit was required for emancipations. [35] The master had to petition for the right to emancipate his slave and state the reasons why he wished to do so. The petition then had to be approved and ratified by a government official. [36] Hostility was expressed toward

---

metropolis his opinion that the American-born white was perfectly capable of working on the sugar estates, and that "the island of Puerto Rico does not need an increase in population because it already contains 500,000 people on a territory of 330 square leagues. . . . Nor is it necessary to increase the number of slaves, already over 50,000 persons; but it is necessary to regulate the class of free day laborers, consisting of over 100,000 people, inspiring them to work in order to supplement the drop in the African slave population." The capitain-general forwarded a proposed law establishing a central registry of day laborers, issuing them identity cards and imposing an annual tax upon them. A.H.N. Ultramar, Legajo 3550, Expediente 16, Raza Blanca y de Color, Carta No. 108, June 12, 1849. For a discussion of forced labor among white settlers of Puerto Rico during the nineteenth century, see Sidney W. Mintz, "Labor and Sugar in Puerto Rico and Jamaica," *Comparative Studies in Society and History* 1, no. 3 (March, 1959):273–83.

[34] *Loix*, Déclaration du Roi, December 15, 1721.

[35] *Loix*, Ordonnance des Administrateurs Généraux des Isles, August 15, 1711; Ordonnance du Roi, October 24, 1713.

[36] *Loix*, Ordonnance de l'Intendant en Fonction, portant concession de la liberté à un de ses esclaves, avec la ratification du général, October 10 and 11, 1721.

testamentary emancipations, on the grounds that sick masters, at the mercy of their slaves, were often forced to emancipate them against their will, and the impatience of the slaves often led them to hasten the death of the master.[37]

A heavy tax was imposed upon emancipations in St. Domingue in 1775: at least 1,000 livres for each male and 2,000 livres for each female under the age of forty was imposed for a permit to emancipate, unless the master could prove extraordinary service to himself or to the colony.[38] Tax-free emancipations were also allowed for military service—such as serving as a drummer in the army for eight years, serving in the Compagnies des Gens Libres for ten years, chasing fugitive slaves, and performing other military duties.[39] There were several examples of slave emancipation for service to the colony, usually the denunciation or capture of fugitive slaves.[40] Slaves were also promised freedom for outstanding acts of bravery on the battlefield.[41]

Growing hostility toward emancipation was again manifested in a steady undercutting of the principle that a slave became free upon touching the soil of France,[42] to the point that by 1762, the institution of slavery had taken root on French soil, and a French court complained: "Paris has become a public market where men are sold to the highest bidder; and there is not a bourgeois, nor a worker, who does not have his black slave."[43]

[37] Petit, *Gouvernement des esclaves*, vol. 2, p. 70.

[38] *Loix*, Ordonnance du Roi, May 22, 1775.

[39] *Loix*, Ordonnance des Administrateurs, October 23, 1775.

[40] For examples, see *Loix*, Arrêt du Conseil du Cap, August 6, 1708; Ordonnance des Administrateurs, February 10, 1710; Ordonnance des Administrateurs, June 28, 1734; Arrêt du Conseil du Cap, July 9, 1750.

[41] For examples, see *Loix*, Arrêt du Conseil de Guerre, February 17, 1695, and Ordonnance des Administrateurs, September 9, 1709.

[42] *Loix*, Extrait de la Lettre du Ministre à M. Ducasse, February 5, 1698; Extrait de la Lettre du Ministre à M. Ducasse, March 11, 1699; Lettre du Ministre sur les Nègres aménes en France, June 10, 1707; Ordonnance du Roi, April 28, 1694; Déclaration du Roi, October 28, 1694; Edit du Roi, October, 1716; Déclaration du Roi, December 15, 1738; Lettre du Ministre aux Administrateurs, June 30, 1763; Règlement du M. l'Intendant, August 29, 1769; Déclaration du Roi, August 9, 1777; Arrêt du Conseil d'Etat, September 7, 1777; Ordonnance du Roi, February 23, 1778.

[43] Paul Trayer, *Etude historique de la condition légale des esclaves dans les colonies françaises* (Paris, 1887), pp. 95, 96.

The Evolution of Spanish Policy toward Emancipation

The Spanish Crown attempted to create a system of forced labor for freedmen as early as the sixteenth century. Collection of tribute became the pretext to force freedmen to live with and work for one master, who became responsible for paying the freedman's tribute from his salary. The freedman could not leave his master's property without a license from the *justicia ordinaria*, and if he left without permission, he could be forcibly returned and imprisoned.[44] Even before the needs of plantation agriculture strongly asserted themselves in the Spanish colonies, the policy was to place the freedmen in villages where they could be supervised and forced to work; this created a special status for freedmen which closely approximated the slave status. The Código Negro Carolino (1785 code) took specific measures to force the free colored population into agricultural labor. It stated that those living freely in the mountains were to move to villages where their actions could be supervised and that they make themselves available for daily employment. Street slaves, except those exploited for the support of the poor, such as minors, widows, and old people, were to be transferred to agricultural labor. Mechanical trades were to be reserved for whites and mestizos.[45] At the height of the slave plantation system in mid-nineteenth century Cuba, any bachelor under the age of fifty who became free and did not, within two months, dedicate himself to labor on a sugar estate was to be permanently deported from the island.[46]

But the simplest and most direct means of maintaining a labor force on the estates was to restrict emancipation, particularly of slaves working in agriculture. And the Código Negro Carolino, mainly concerned with promoting a plantation system in the Spanish Caribbean, severely restricted emancipation. "Since liberty is the greatest recompense for slaves, there will be few acts worthy of it." Emancipation was to be allowed only for limited reasons: for example, denunciation of a conspiracy, saving the life of a white person, being the mother of six children over seven years of age, thirty years of faithful service, etc. Self-purchase (*coartación*) was severely limited. "To prevent theft, masters are forbidden the unlimited faculty of

---

[44] *DHFS*, vol. 1, pp. 502, 503.
[45] C.N.C., Cap. 50, 51, 54, and 55.
[46] A.H.N. Ultramar, Legajo 4655, Expediente 181.

conferring liberty only for the obligation of a price." The slave could not solicit his freedom "without justifying extrajudically and instructively his good conduct and procedures, and the means by which he acquired the quantity offered; requirements which the justices shall not dispense with even upon the petition of his own master." A government permit was required for emancipations, even testamentary ones. The Code provided for reenslavement of the "freedman who is in grave default of gratitude to his master, or the wife or children of his master" and applied his price to charity.[47]

THE IMPACT OF THE HAITIAN REVOLUTION UPON RACIAL POLICIES IN NINETEENTH-CENTURY CUBA

Colonial officials were fairly competent comparative historians, and avidly sought to learn the lessons of the Haitian Revolution to prevent a repetition of similar scenes on their own soil. The archives are full of admonitions and suggestions about how to prevent another Santo Domingo. The initial response of officials to the Haitian Revolution was to try to isolate Cuban slaves from slaves who might be infected with revolutionary sentiments. Slaves coming from other colonies in the Americas were prohibited from entering Cuba; only newly arrived Africans were allowed. Slaves who had arrived from the French colonies since 1790 and from the English colonies since 1794 were to be deported. Because of the lack of boats to deport them, however, many were held in jail.[48]

The progress of the Haitian Revolution was carefully followed in Cuba. Official communications contained detailed reports about the fighting. General Rigaud appealed for help from the Spanish authorities in Cuba after he had been forced to evacuate the southern part of St. Domingue and leave Toussaint l'Ouverture in full possession. Refugees, including General Rigaud's faction, began arriving. The General was to be interned separately from his followers, and ordered to have nothing to do with, and not to communicate with, any colored Cuban. He was not to remain in Cuba but

[47] C.N.C., Cap. 103, 104, 105, 106, 107, 110, and 116.
[48] A.H.N. Estado, Legajo 6366, No. 1, Carta de Marqués de Somerueles, January 27, 1800, referring to the prohibition of the entrance of foreign slaves in accordance with a *Bando* of January 15, 1796, promulgated by Captain-General Don Luis de las Cases.

was to be sent to Spain. Madrid ordered the captain-general to refuse to allow ships carrying colored refugees from St. Domingue to land. They were to offer the ships whatever provisions they needed so they could leave as soon as possible because "in no manner is the entrance of more colored people convenient."[49]

French immigration to Cuba from St. Domingue had reached 18,213 by January 31, 1804. Aside from these permanent settlers, French troops, many of them sick, were evacuated to Cuba.[50] It was the French immigrants from St. Domingue who developed the Cuban coffee industry. But even more important, they served as a constant reminder of the possibilities of insurrection by the slaves and the free colored population.

On March 21, 1809, there was a riot against the French immigrants as a reaction to the French occupation of Spain. Several officers of the Batallon de Pardos y Morenos, who were later implicated in the Aponte Conspiracy, took an active part in the rioting.[51] Aponte himself consulted with Gil Narciso, a Haitian general in 1811, who explained how the Haitians had gotten arms, and agreed to take command once the colored Cubans secured arms.[52] The Cabildos of the Carabalis in Bayamo used symbols of the Haitian Revolution. They placed a Haitian bicorn on their flag instead of the Spanish Crown, used the colors of the Haitian flag, and wore hats like those of the Haitian generals and officials and black feathers like those of Haitian magistrates.[53] Aponte contacted white abolitionists, Cuban *independistas*, and groups of free blacks and slaves in North America, Santo Domingo, Haiti, and Brazil, and urged them to join his conspiracy.[54]

In view of the decisive role played by the colored elite of St. Domingue in initiating the Haitian Revolution, Cuban officials were determined to stifle the wealthy and educated colored elite of Cuba. Destruction of this segment of Cuban society was ruthlessly carried out during the suppression of the Conspiracy of the Ladder through mass executions and deporta-

---

[49] A.H.N. Estado, Legajo 6366, No. 1, Communications during the year 1800.

[50] A.H.N. Estado, Legajo 6366, No. 2, Comunicación del Gobernador Marqués de Somerueles, January, 1804.

[51] José L. Franco, *La conspiración de Aponte*, ser. 53 (Havana: Publicaciones del Archivo Nacional, 1963), p. 17.

[52] *Ibid.*, p. 53.

[53] *Ibid.*, p. 55.

[54] *Ibid.*, p. 53.

tions. Remnants of this class were dispersed to neighboring countries. Over 200 free colored Cubans were interned in Mexico "after the insult which said blacks and mulattoes had offered to the Consul of His Majesty at Veracruz, below whose windows they shouted tumultuously, during the night of the fifteenth of September, 'Death to the Spaniards, death to the tyrants!'" The consul was advised not to consider them Spanish citizens, nor give any visa or passport to any colored person to go to the island of Cuba.[55] In January 1845, the Spanish Minister to Mexico informed his government that the colored residents of Vera Cruz had formed a junta which, in league with one in New York, was organizing a conspiracy to assassinate the whites of Cuba at the rate of one a day. O'Donnell wrote "regardless of how senseless and barbarous this plan seems, all is believable of such savages. I am informed that it is horrifying to listen to their discussions about exterminating the Island." Their information was that the junta in Mexico was well supplied with money from New York. And although the colored Cubans had been ordered to be interned at ten leagues from the coast, "I do not consider this sufficient, because all of them are bad."[56]

GROWING HOSTILITY TOWARD THE FREE COLORED POPULATION IN NINETEENTH-CENTURY CUBA

By the early nineteenth century, Spain had lost her far-flung empire in America, and Cuba had lost her strategic importance at the same time that her economic role became vital. The drastic reduction in the size of the Spanish Empire allowed Spain to concentrate her military forces in Cuba, and a large, standing army of Spanish troops minimized the military role of the free colored population at the same time that the needs of plantation agriculture demanded a sharp restriction upon emancipation of estate slaves. There was, nevertheless, a large free colored population which had arisen out of the essentially strategic needs of the previous centuries.

Official hostility toward emancipation of slaves and toward the free

[55] A.H.N. Estado, Legajo 8039, Carta del Ministro Español a México al Sec. de Estado, October 24, 1844.

[56] A.H.N. Estado, Legajo 8039, No. 87, Carta del Ministro Español a México al Sec. de Estado, January 4, 1845; Carta del Capitan-General O'Donnell al Consul Español en Veracruz, November 5, 1844.

colored population reached extreme proportions during the nineteenth century. In 1832, for example, the king of Spain asked the captain-general of Cuba "if the existence of the free colored population is convenient, and what rules are most desirable for their expulsion in the negative case, or what rules for the security of the Island in the affirmative?" The captain-general responded:

Since the mistake of not limiting emancipations has already been made . . . and the mistake has been further aggravated by viewing with indifference the propagation of the free colored population, it would be very imprudent to try to correct omissions and defects which can only be deplored, because [it is inadvisable to take measures] without committing injustices which would arouse discontent and inevitably lead to the ruin of the country.[57]

The entire free colored population was held in distrust. "The existence of free blacks and mulattoes in the midst of the slavery of their companions is an example which will become very dangerous one day." The free colored population was divided into two groups. The most dangerous were those who "if not by true intention, at least by their stolid perversity," were most suspect. Most of them lived "submerged in vices, have bad habits, and have all the dispositions to launch themselves in a criminal career." The second group were "honest artisans, good fathers of families, owning land and slaves." Although they were counted upon to maintain public order, it was not advisable to "expose the virtues of these men to heroic proofs," since they could very well be carried along in a unified revolutionary movement of the colored people, and should therefore be considered as "indirectly dangerous."[58]

Draconian measures were taken to prevent immigration of free colored people into Cuba. By a royal order of March 12, 1837, all free persons of color were prohibited from landing under any pretext whatsoever. Anyone landing in Cuba or Puerto Rico who was suspected, no matter how remotely, of African descent, and whatever his complexion, was committed to prison. Free colored seamen on their arrival were removed from their

[57] Un interrogatorio absuelto por el Capitan-General don Francisco Dionisio Vives, published in José Antonio Saco, *Historia de la esclavitud de la raza africana en el Nuevo Mundo y en especial en los países américo-hispanos*, 4 vols. (Havana: Cultural S.A., 1938), 4:341–56.
[58] *Ibid.*, pp. 353–54.

ships and imprisoned until their ships were ready to depart, when they were again put on board and compelled to leave the island.

Lord Clarendon, British Minister to Spain, asked the Spanish government whether it could be necessary that men who, in their own country, enjoyed every privilege to which their fellow citizens were entitled, should, on their reaching the shores of Cuba, be treated as if they brought with them some physical or moral pestilence.[59] A communication from the French government dating from the late 1850s requested that colored crew members be allowed to debark in Havana, or stay abroad ship without posting a large bond.[60]

The Conspiracy of the Ladder, whether real, imaginary, or exaggerated, resulted in extreme intensification of official hostility toward the free colored population of Cuba. A report dating from May, 1844, warned against the possibility of becoming the "sad victim" of this class of population which, like a true social *superfetación* (literally, a pregnancy when pregnancy already exists) was in contact with both free and slave and aspired to the privileges of the free citizen. Having slave origins, the free colored were generally corrupt even though they had some education. It was claimed that the free colored population originated from the city slaves "by which our houses are plagued. These domestics, living in comfort and at times in luxury, in absolute control of their time, can easily, by more or less legitimate means, free themselves and their families, thus multiplying this flood of free people of color who are so abundant in the cities." It was estimated that the free colored and slave population was already, perhaps, numerically superior to the white population, and that the free colored population increased naturally twice as fast as the white population, "as can be verified by the number of baptisms recorded each year."[61]

Captain-General O'Donnell pointed out that the free colored population would not work on the sugar estates and was not, in general, favorable to the development of the island, nor to its security and tranquility. Some dedicated themselves to industrial occupations; the rest, lazy but intelligent

---

[59] David Turnbull, *Travels in the West Indies* (London, 1840), pp. 69, 70.

[60] A.H.N. Estado, Legajo 8048, Suelta.

[61] A.H.N. Ultramar, Legajo 3551, Expediente formado para imponer una capitación sobre los esclavos del servicio doméstico, Informes de Escmo. Sr. Conde de Cañongo, Joaquim Santos Juarez, y Antonio Mª de Esconedo, May 20, 1844.

enough to desire the comforts of life, became ambitious and disposed toward disorder and revolution. The problem was more acute among the *mulatos* and *pardos libres*, because of their greater intelligence and ambition. Some of them had become mixed up with whites, enjoyed the greatest social considerations, and wished to break the bonds that prevented them from enjoying rank and position.[62]

The Cuban authorities embarked on a deliberate policy of "reducing the numerous free colored population by all possible means."

If their presence was always highly prejudicial, it is even more so since the last conspiracy projected on the territory of Matanzas, in which they played a big role. The Superior Authorities of the Island have repeatedly clamored for the necessity of this measure, always recognizing that it could not be violent because of the great number of individuals involved, because they possess some means, and because the general attention of the entire world is fixed upon our conduct with our *pardos* and *negros* of all conditions.

Taking into consideration that "the Spanish character should never lose its proverbial reputation for justice and equity," the Sección de Ultramar concluded that it should take measures to only "alleviate this bad condition, without prejudice to acting otherwise if the circumstances demand it." The decision was to promote massive deportation of the free colored population of Cuba on an individual basis. The Captain-General and the Tribunals of Cuba were instructed to pronounce sentences of deportation against "all free colored persons who by their conduct give reason to believe that they are prejudicial to the repose of the country." And since it was not possible to deny in law the right of slaves to emancipation, they were given the choice of either remaining slaves or dedicating themselves to labor on a sugar estate. Otherwise, they would be deported.[63]

The captain-general ordered the expulsion of all *negros y mulatos libres* who came to Cuba from other countries when they were adults. It was proposed that any slave purchasing his freedom should be given it only on the condition that he leave the country and that those free blacks who did

[62] A.H.N. Ultramar, Legajo 3550, Expediente 16, No. 854, Carta de Capitan-General O'Donnell al Sec. de Estado, November 10, 1847.

[63] A.H.N. Ultramar, Legajo 4655, Expediente 181, No. 9, Carta de Marcelino Oracio al Sec. de Estado, December 22, 1846.

not come from foreign countries should be subjected to a severe vigilance. The British consul strongly protested these measures.[64]

A Bando de la Policía Municipal ordered the apprehension of all "delinquents, including vagrants and idlers" and strict vigilance of any meeting of more than two people, whether they be slaves or free colored people. Prohibition against the entrance of any colored person coming from a foreign country was reiterated, and those already in Cuba who had not come from Africa had to leave. No free colored male, whether Cuban or African born, between the ages of twenty and sixty, could remain in Cuba. Special exception could be made by proving to the satisfaction of the governor that the man was married, had children of his marriage, regularly exercised a trade or had a private capital of 30,000 pesos, had good habits, was submissive to the government, and had not been involved in seditious plots. All violators of the aforesaid two articles were to be interned in a camp set up for that purpose. No slave could acquire freedom in the future except by leaving Cuba, and would not enjoy freedom without complying with that condition.[65] An Instruction dating from May, 1844, ordered a roundup of all *emancipados* (see the following section) who had "terminated their civil and religious teaching and instruction" so that they could be expelled from the Island. A census of all free colored men who lived in Cuba and had no trade, property, or known means of livelihood was to be made, so that they could be sentenced by the *tribunal privativo de vagos* as prejudicial to society. Free colored people coming from any other country were to be expelled within a given time. The prohibition against the landing of any *gente de color*, free or slave, was to be vigorously enforced.[66]

The Spanish authorities made it known that those free colored people leaving Cuba would not be allowed to return under any circumstances. The

---

[64] A.H.N. Estado, Legajo 8039, Expediente general de negros, Expediente de la insurrección de Matanzas: Puntos acerca de los cuales ha pedido instrucciones el Capitan-General de la Isla de Cuba (sin fecha).

[65] A.H.N. Estado, Legajo 8039, No. 55, Título 3 de la policía municipal, Capítulo 1°, De la policía de seguridad (sin fecha), Articles 14, 129, 130, 131, and 132. Cover letter from Captain General O'Donnell dated June 15, 1844.

[66] Providencias de 31 de mayo, 1844, Articles 1, 2, 3, and 4, recommended by the *Junta de Fomento* and given the force of law by Captain-General O'Donnell. Published in Don José Ferrer de Couto, *Los negros en sus diversos estados y condiciones; tales como son, como se supone que son, y como deben ser*, 2d ed. (New York: Hallet Press, 1864), pp. 80–83.

following announcement was published in the *New York Herald* on October 9, 1844:

His excellency, the Captain-General of the Island of Cuba, has addressed me the following official letter, dated the 31st of August last: Spontaneously, and by petition of the parties concerned, I have granted passports to several individuals of color, who have solicited them for different parts out of this Island. On delivering to them said documents, they have been particularly warned that, by a general rule, all people of color are prohibited from entering the territory of this Island. In consequence whereof, to prevent the expenses and injuries that must devolve on those who should now or hereafter intend to return, or who should propose settling themselves in the Island at any time, I have deemed it expedient to communicate these facts to your Excellency, in order not to authorize the granting of passports to any person of color whatever; for by the ordinances in force, they cannot be admitted therein. Signed F. Stoughton, Consul of Spain.[67]

A pass system for the entire free colored population of Cuba was ordered in 1855. By 1857, a register was set up, and every man, woman, and child had to pay a fixed annual sum for his identity card.[68]

THE "EMANCIPADOS"

Hostility toward emancipation in nineteenth-century Cuba was clearly manifested in the treatment of the so-called *emancipados*, who were Africans seized by the British from ships engaged in the slave trade once it had been outlawed by international treaty. Considerable discussion took place concerning the disposition of these Africans. In 1825, 150 Africans were confiscated from a slave trade ship. They were given certificates of emancipation, and distributed as freedmen among *vecinos* (citizens) and *hacendados* (landowners). Fear was expressed of the "transcendental and fatal consequences which could result in this Island if all the free blacks remain in it."[69] A Consulta del Consejo de las Indias recommended that the *emancipados* be sent to southern Spain.[70]

---

[67] A.H.N. Estado, Legajo 8039, No. 29, Clipping of announcement in the *New York Herald* of October 9, 1844.

[68] A.H.N. Ultramar, Legajo 4655, Expediente 183, *Sobre modificación de las cédulas de los libres de color*, Census of March 2, 1858.

[69] A.H.N. Ultramar, Legajo 3548–49, Informe de la Contaduría general, March 4, 1825.

[70] A.H.N. Ultramar, Legajo 3548–49, Consulta del Consejo de Ministros, March 18 and April 14, 1825.

The advantages and disadvantages of keeping the *emancipados* in Cuba were weighed. On the one hand, a class distinct from the slaves would be created, and by thus dividing "the interests of one and the other, this very inequality is the strongest stimulus to encourage servitude." On the other hand,

if those who have redeemed themselves from slavery by their honor, or by their savings which has been the fruit of proper conduct are feared in the towns because of their excessive numbers compared to the whites, how much more are they to be feared if we add to them *negros bozales* who lack these qualities? And how much greater would be the danger if the incendiary spirit of Independence is communicated to the slaves, making a common cause, following the example of those of Santo Domingo?

Official anxiety was expressed over the introduction of *emancipados* into Santiago de Cuba in spite of the fact that only one-third of its population was white, the other two-thirds was colored, and the situation was already considered extremely aggravated because half of the colored population was free.[71] The Consejo de las Indias, meeting in 1825, concluded that it was too dangerous to the tranquility of Cuba for the *emancipados* to remain, and ordered that they be sent back to Africa, or to the British possessions.[72] Apparently, this decision was not enforced, and in 1829, the king ordered that all the *emancipados* be removed from Cuba and taken to "any of the possessions of His Majesty in Europe, even to the Peninsula. . . ."[73] The latter decision was not implemented either, and in 1832, the captain-general communicated to the Secretary of State "the incalculable prejudice caused to the Island by the *negros emancipados*," and the necessity of expelling them, and asked for a ship to be used for this purpose.[74]

But the presence of the *emancipados* in Cuba proved to be very profitable to certain governmental officials. They were forced to work on "contract" for a period of seven years, their wages going to the benefit of "public works." When their contract time was up, if they had survived, they were normally resold for another seven years. It was impossible for

[71] A.H.N. Ultramar, Legajo 3548–49, Carta de Manuel Ximenez Guarzo, October 12, 1825; Despacho, November 20, 1825.

[72] A.H.N. Ultramar, Legajo, 3548–49, Consulta de Consejo de las Indias, November 17, 1825.

[73] A.H.N. Ultramar, Legajo 3548–49, Despacho, July 21, 1829.

[74] A.H.N. Estado, Legajo 6338³, No. 6, Carta del Capitan-General al Sec. de Estado, May, 1832; No. 13, June, 1832.

these so-called *emancipados* to obtain their freedom, even by paying the price asked for their contract. "The Government refuses to give it to them. Several of them, having offered the price that any other person would pay to have the *emancipado* in his service, received the answer that their proposition would be entertained if they returned themselves to Africa."[75]

Captain-General Valdès, who was reputed to be the only captain-general who did not exact his ounce of gold for every slave illegally imported into Cuba, aside from significantly reducing the African slave trade, tried to end the official exploitation of the *emancipados* by giving them certificates of emancipation (*cartas de libertad*) on a large scale. Valdès believed that all the *emancipados* should be freed within five years.[76] His successor, Captain-General O'Donnell, reduced the issuance of *cartas de libertad* "which were so profusely conceded by my antecessor to the *emancipados*," recalling that he had recommended, as one of the most important means of assuring the tranquility of Cuba, the expulsion of the *emancipados* who declared themselves free, and of "all those who abuse this grace by their bad ideas or conduct," so as not to increase the numbers of the free colored class, and especially those coming from the *emancipados*, who, he claimed, contributed most to the unrest among the estate slaves with which they were mixed. Captain-General O'Donnell ordered the suspension of the issuance of *cartas de libertad* to the *emancipados*, and inquired what was to be done, not only with the *emancipados*, but also with the free blacks and mulattoes who "by the faults they commit, their bad conduct or ideas and tendencies contrary to the tranquility and security of this country, should be exiled and returned to Africa, to the Peninsula, or handed over to the English."[77]

The following population figures reflect the growing hostility toward emancipation in Cuba with the rise of the plantation system.[78] Note that there was an absolute decline in the free colored population between 1817 and 1827, and again between 1841 and 1846, the latter period the years

[75] Interrogatorio de R. R. Madden, absuelto en 17 de septiembre de 1839 por Domingo Delmonte, published in Saco, *Historia de la esclavitud*, vol. 4, pp. 330–40.
[76] A.H.N. Estado, Legajo 8038, Suelta.
[77] A.H.N. Estado, Legajo 8055, Expediente 31, Carta de O'Donnell al Prin. Sec. de Estado; A.H.N. Estado, Legajo 8039, No. 77, Carta de O'Donnell al Sec. de. Estado, September 27, 1844.
[78] Ortiz, *Los negros esclavos*, pp. 321, 322.

of the suppression of the Conspiracy of the Ladder.[79] The *emancipados*, averaging about 25,000, were counted among the free population.

Year	Slaves	Percentage	Free	Percentage
1774	44,333	59.0	30,847	41.0
1792	64,590	54.4	54,151	45.6
1817	199,292	63.3	115,691	36.7
1827	286,942	72.9	106,494	27.1
1830	310,978	73.5	112,365	26.5
1841	436,495	74.1	152,838	25.9
1846	323,759	68.5	149,226	31.5
1849	324,187	66.3	164,712	33.7
1855	366,421	67.2	179,012	32.8
1858	364,253	67.5	175,274	32.5
1860	367,758	63.7	209,407	36.3
1861	377,203	62.9	225,843	37.4
1872	379,523	61.7	235,938	38.3
1877	199,094	44.3	272,478	55.7

Considering that colonial officials were constantly complaining about the high birthrate among the free colored population of Cuba, it appears likely that draconian measures against the free colored population in nineteenth-century Cuba was one aspect of Spanish law that was diligently enforced. The evidence would indicate that a preexisting racial attitude of the people of the colonizing nations was not the crucial factor in determining policy toward emancipation of the slaves and the status of the free colored population, but the crucial factors were the sharp internal and external conflicts and tensions which beset these colonial societies.

[79] Fernando Ortiz, *La hampa afro-cubana: Los negros esclavos* (Havana: Ruiz y Cª, 1916), p. 434; Klein, *Slavery in the Americas*, p. 221.

VII

RACISM AS AN INSTRUMENT OF
SOCIAL AND POLITICAL
DOMINATION

As THE SLAVE population began decisively to outnumber the white population in the countryside, the obvious symbol of visible racial differences was seized upon as a means of convincing the slaves of their own innate inferiority. Overt racist policies were instituted during the last half of the eighteenth century in St. Domingue, and perhaps because this period preceded the flowering of racist theories during the nineteenth century as the institution of slavery itself was seriously challenged, French ideologists did not find it necessary to attempt to convince themselves of the innate inferiority of the Africans. They contented themselves with trying to convince the Africans. Containing the slaves and maintaining the social order were frankly acknowledged as the reason for racist policies. A Memoire du Roi dating from 1777 was blunt.

Whatever distance they may be from their origin, they always keep the stain of slavery, and are declared incapable of all public functions. Even gentlemen with the slightest trace of Negro blood cannot enjoy the prerogatives of nobility. This law is harsh, but wise and necessary. In a country where there are 15 slaves to 1 white, one cannot put too much distance between the two species, one cannot impress upon the blacks too much respect for those they serve. This distinction, rigorously observed even after freedom, is the principal prop of the subordination of the slave, that results from the opinion that his color is inextricably linked with servitude, and nothing can render him equal to his master.[1]

[1] Quoted in Antoine Gisler, *L'Esclavage aux antilles française (XVIIe–XIXe siècles): Contribution au problème de l'esclavage* (Fribourg: Editions Universitaires Fribourg Suisse, 1964), pp. 99, 100.

Hilliard d'Auberteuil explained that "interest and security demand that we overwhelm the Black race with so much disdain that whoever descends from it until the sixth generation shall be covered by an indelible stain."[2] The very spectacle of free blacks was dangerous for slaves, since color should be absolutely identified with the slave status.[3]

In nineteenth-century Cuba, however, the ideologists of racism were already infected with belief in the inherent racial inferiority of the blacks.

In dealing with the emancipation of our slaves, one deals not only with altering a social relationship, undermining a law which subjects one man to another, destroying the sole distinction which existed between them, but with placing a black and a white on a plane of legal equality, uniting with social ties two races which have imprinted on their faces an indelible mark of physical and moral separation which only immorality and vice, and then only rarely, unite, and it is absolutely essential that the one command and the other obey.[4]

Spain always had a policy of racial separation in the Americas, the ideal being separate communities of Blacks, Indians, and Spaniards. But it was impossible to prevent biological merger on a large scale among the three races.[5] Discrimination against people of African origin in any degree became even stronger during the latter half of the eighteen century,[6] a development confirmed by the record of cases acted upon by the Consejo de las Indias during this period.[7]

As plantation agriculture flourished, along with the tendency to restrict emancipation, identify blackness with slavery, and degrade the free colored population there was also a tendency to create a caste system that fomented

[2] Hilliard d'Auberteuil, *Considerations sur l'état présent de la colonie française de St. Domingue*, 2 vols. (Paris, 1776–77), 2:73.

[3] *Ibid.*, vol. 2, p. 84.

[4] El tribunal de Comercio de esta plaza de la Habana, representa a la Regencia del reino contra el emancipación de los esclavos de esta Isla, fecha 30 de marzo de 1841, extendida por el Sr. Intendente don Wenceslao de Villaurrutía, published in José Antonio Saco, *Historia de la esclavitud de la raza africana en el Nuevo Mundo y en especial en los países américo-hispanos*, 4 vols. (Havana: Cultural S.A., 1938), 4:136–53.

[5] Rolondo Mellafe, *La esclavitud en Hispanoamérica* (Buenos Aires: Eudeba Editorial Universitaria de Buenos Aires, 1964), p. 87.

[6] Magnus Mörner, *Race Mixture in the History of Latin America* (Boston: Little, Brown and Co., 1967), p. 45.

[7] See *DHFS*, vol. 2, p. 247; vol. 3, pp. 265–66; vol. 3, pp. 287–92; vol. 3, pp. 318–19; vol. 3, pp. 594–96; vol. 3, pp. 625–26.

mutual antagonisms among people of varing degrees of African descent by establishing distinct legal and social categories according to the percentage of admixture of European blood, the number of generations of legitimate birth, and the number of generations removed from slavery. A clear-cut caste system was formulated in Spanish law as part of the Bourbon Reform movement encouraging plantation agriculture. The Código Negro Carolino (1785 code) established a complex social caste system among people of varying degrees of African descent. "It is necessary to divide the races and generations for the just regulation of the status they should have in the public order and the occupations and trades to which these classes shall be destined." The population was divided into blacks, both slave and free. The free were divided into blacks and mulattoes or *pardos*. The legitimate children of a white man and black woman were considered the first generation. The children born from a legitimate marriage of a legitimate *pardo* and a white were the second generation; those born to a member of the second generation and a white were known as *tercerones*. The child of the marriage of a *terceron* with a white person person would be considered a *cuarteron*, and a child of the next generation would be called a *mestizo* (from the French term, *metif*). The sixth legitimate generation of this whitening process would be considered white, if the order had not been interrupted, in which case the process would revert to the status of the person who interrupted the process.[8]

Luxurious dress was forbidden to *negros y pardos primeros*. Elementary and religious schools were also to be closed to them, since they were destined for agricultural labor. Submissiveness toward all whites was encouraged. "No *negro, pardo, cuarteron*, nor *mestizo* can question or contradict, except in very submissive terms, white people, even if they know they are right, nor raise their voice with elation and pride under penalties of public humiliation or prison, depending upon the 'generation' of the culprit." The first generation was to constitute the equilibrium between the white and black population, making the latter submissive and respectful, since experience in all the colonies had proved that the mulattoes "never mixed with the blacks (whom they regard with aversion), in their up-

[8] C.N.C., Cap. 14.

risings, flights, and attempts against the state, and were the strongest prop of public authority." [9] It is clear, then, that absolute devaluation of African descent and glorification of white descent was deliberately promoted by the authorities as a means of maintaining the stability of the system.

Origin of the Colored Elite of St. Domingue

There was a sharp contrast between the early egalitarian policies toward race and the discriminatory policies characteristic of the late colonial period in St. Domingue. The Code Noir guaranteed in unequivocal language full citizenship rights to slaves emancipated in the French islands, and treated them as native-born French citizens regardless of where they had been born.[10] These measures were no doubt motivated by the desire to count as many heads as possible at a time when the principle of effective occupation determined control of the islands, and the small population and the military use to which slaves and freedmen were put encouraged an equalitarian atmosphere. The population factor, especially the shortage of white women, was certainly very important in promoting racial equality in early St. Domingue.[11] Dutertre wrote:

There are many mulattoes in the Islands who are free and work for themselves. I have seen some fairly handsome ones who have married Frenchmen. This disorder was previously more common than it is today, when the number of women and girls in the Antilles prevent it; but at the beginning of colonization, it was terrible and almost without remedy.[12]

---

[9] C.N.C., Cap. 65, 66, 19, 24, and 16.

[10] Articles 57, 58, and 59. Article 59 reads, "We give to the freedmen the same rights, privileges, and immunities enjoyed by free-born persons; we will that the merit of an acquired liberty produce in them the same effects upon their persons as well as their property as the good fortune of natural freedom causes to our other subjects." Later versions of the Code Noir sometimes read, "Voulons qu'ils méritent une liberté acquise," but this is an inaccuracy stemming from the growth of racism. The original Code Noir reads, "Voulons que la mérite d'une liberté acquise."

[11] For some interesting concepts about the impact of population patterns on racial attitudes and organization of colonial society, see Marvin Harris, *Patterns of Race in the Americas* (New York: Walker, 1964); and Winthrop D. Jordan, "American Chiaroscuro: The Status and Definition of Mulattoes in the British Colonies," *William and Mary Quarterly* 19, no. 2 (April, 1962): 183–200.

[12] Jean-Baptiste Dutertre, *Histoire générales des antilles habitées par les françois,* 4 vols. (Paris, 1667–71), 2:513.

Interracial unions, both informal and legalized, continued on a large scale throughout the history of the colony. Article 9 of the Code Noir exerted pressure on the master to marry his slave concubine, thereby freeing her and legitimizing their children, under penalty of fine and confiscation of the concubine family, who could thereafter never be freed. Before the promulgation of the Code Noir, it was accepted that the offspring of unions between white men and black women were automatically emancipated when they reached the age of twenty-one. The Code Noir followed the Roman principle that the status of the newborn child was the same as the mother's and thereafter formal emancipation in writing became necessary. Dissatisfaction was expressed with this provision, and in 1697, an official proposed a law declaring all mulattoes free as soon as they reached the age of twenty-one. The Minister agreed to propose such a change in the Code Noir "which was formulated without having examined this question in depth."[13] It is evident that Article 9 was frequently violated. Many children were emancipated because they were "children of free men." This would have been legal only if the father was not the master, or if the master had married his slave concubine.[14]

There was strong sentiment in favor of the emancipation of the natural children of the master throughout the history of the colony, and these children were an important source of the free colored population. As late as 1735, mulattoes were specifically excluded from the policy of sharply restricting the emancipation of slaves. The colonial authorities were instructed, "You should not follow the same policy with the mulattoes. I know that they are the declared enemies of the blacks."[15] As late as 1777, Emilien Petit favored freedom for the mulatto children of white planters and making the fathers responsible for their care until they came of age, because

it is to the affection of their concubines that whites have owed the discovery of several conspiracies. . . . The children born of these concubinages

---

[13] *Loix*, Extrait de la Lettre du Ministre à M. Ducasse, February 5, 1698.
[14] Lucien Peytraud, *L'Esclavage aux antilles françaises avant 1789* (Paris, 1897), p. 199.
[15] *Loix*, Extrait de la Lettre à M. le Marquis de Fayet, March 29, 1735.

form a class of freedmen who are always distinguished from the other classes of free colored people, with which they have few ties, and whom they despise. The freedman who depends upon his master or patron for his subsistence will not easily risk seeing himself deprived of it. One would find fewer guilty parties among the mulattoes if they had something to lose.[16]

Race mixture was not discouraged in pre-plantation St. Domingue. The Code Noir was not concerned about preventing the fusion of the races, either physically or legally.[17] A judgment rendered by the Conseil de la Martinique in 1698 declared that the Code Noir aimed only at the vice of concubinage. Far from preventing race mixture (*le mélange des sangs*), it was concerned only with augmenting the colony, and exempted the master who married his slave concubine from paying the fine.[18] As late as 1713, the administrators were remarkably free from preoccupation with *le mélange des sangs* that was typical of the late colony. Pointing to widespread concubinage of slave women, they complained that masters kept their concubines and their children openly in their homes, "exposing them to the eyes of all with as much assurance as if they had been procreated from a legitimate marriage."[19]

Throughout the history of the colony, whether by virtue of the provisions of the Code Noir or otherwise, legal intermarriage was far from unusual in St. Domingue. The king refused, in 1703, to receive the titles of nobility of several French noblemen because they had married *mulatresses*.[20] A report dating from 1731 indicated that intermarriage was almost universal in some parts of St. Domingue. "In the inspection which M. de la Roch-Allard has made in Cayes in the neighborhood of Jacumel, he reported to me that there are few whites of pure blood. . . . The whites ally themselves willingly in marriage with the blacks, because the latter, through their frugality, acquire property more easily than the whites."[21]

---

[16] Emilien Petit, *Traité sur le gouvernement des esclaves*, 2 vols. (Paris: Knapen, 1777), 2:72–75.
[17] Peytraud, *L'Esclavage aux antilles française*, p. 156.
[18] *Ibid.*, p. 202.
[19] *Loix*, Ordonnance des Administrateurs, December 18, 1713.
[20] *Loix*, Lettre du Ministre au Gouverneur Général des Isles.
[21] Peytraud, *L'Esclavage aux antilles françaises*, p. 207.

A nephew and cousin tried unsuccessfully in 1746 to prevent their white relative's marriage with a *mulatresse*. The court ordered the publication of the bans, and the curé to proceed with the marriage under penalty of seizure of his stipend.[22]

Marriage between white masters and their slave concubines and between impecunious white Frenchmen and financially comfortable women of color were common enough to inspire bitter comments during the last few decades of the colony. Hilliard d'Auberteuil wrote that the Code Noir "is subject to great abuse."

> How many *Negresses* have profited from it and appropriated the entire fortune of their masters, brutalized by libertinage, and incapable of resisting their power over feeble and seduced souls. . . . The wealth of families has been sacrificed to passion, has become the price of debauchery, and respectable names have fallen, along with the best lands, to legitimized mulattoes.[23]

White men who married *filles de couleur* were accused of doing so for money. There were about 300 white men, several gentlemen by birth, who were married to *sang-mêlées*. "They make these women whom cupidity has induced them to marry miserable; their children incapable of filling any civil function, and condemned to share the humiliation of slaves."[24] Emilien Petit favored outlawing intermarriage under penalty of nullification, a prohibition which was "necessary to prevent unions so contrary to the growth of the white population, and to maintain the superiority of white blood, which such misalliances degrade."[25]

The wealth of the free colored population was a unique feature of St. Domingue. The Code Noir placed no restrictions upon inheritance of property, and the offspring of alliances between master and slave, whether legitimate or not, freely inherited their fathers' property, land and slaves. Abrogating the Code Noir in this respect, an Ordonnance du Roi dating from 1726 declared that free blacks, their children, and descendants were incapable in the future of receiving any donation from whites before or

---

[22] *Loix*, Arrêt du Conseil du Cap, May 2 and June 13, 1746.
[23] Hilliard d'Auberteuil, *Considerations sur l'état*, vol. 1, pp. 80, 81.
[24] *Ibid.*, vol. 2, p. 79, 79 n.
[25] Petit, *Gouvernement des esclaves*, vol. 2, p. 81.

after their death, under penalty of confiscation of the property.[26] But this change came too late for St. Domingue, and the decree was never enforced in the colony.[27]

The courts of St. Domingue consistently awarded contested legacies to the colored offspring of white masters. There was a case in which the party who was to inherit an estate in the event that the deceased left no legitimate posterity denied that a former slave wife of the deceased and their legitimized children constituted legitimate posterity. The lower court held for the mulatto children; the Conseil du Cap reversed the lower court, but the Conseil d'Etat reversed the Conseil du Cap in 1772, giving the inheritance to the mulatto children.[28] A judgment dating from 1775 awarded two estates and 240 slaves to the mulatto bastards of a white father who had willed this property to them.[29] A judgment dating from 1782 awarded half of the inheritance to the brothers and sisters of the deceased, and half to the children of Nanette Soreau, *mulatresse libre*, in accordance with the terms of the deceased's will.[30]

The free colored population increased rapidly, despite restrictions upon emancipation and social degradation enacted during the last half of the eighteenth century. The census listed 500 *gens de couleur libres* around 1700. By 1715, their number had increased to 1,500. By 1780, the figure reached 28,000. Between 1770 and 1780, there were 7,000 to 8,000 individual emancipations in the colony, and marriages among *affranchis*, slaves, and French colonists were never more common.[31] It appears that the free colored elite was moving rapidly toward outnumbering, if not absorbing, the white elite during the last few years of the colony. The

[26] *Loix*, Déclaration du Roi, February 8, 1726; C. Vanufel et Champion de Villeneuve, *Codes des Colons de St. Domingue* (Paris: MᵉVergne, 1826), pp. 42, 43.

[27] Auguste Lebeau, *De la condition des gens de couleur libres sous l'Ancien Régime d'après des documents des archives coloniales* (Paris: Guillaumin et Cⁱᵉ, 1903), p. 15.

[28] *Loix*, Arrêt du Conseil du Cap, December 21, 1769.

[29] *Loix*, Arrêt du Conseil du Cap, October 5, 1775.

[30] *Loix*, Arrêt du Conseil du Cap, April 29, 1782.

[31] M. L. E. Moreau de St.-Méry, *Description topographique, physique, civile, politique, et historique de la partie française de l'Isle Saint-Domingue*, 4 vols. (Philadelphia, 1797), 1:68.

figures below that refer to whites and free colored are for persons owning property or slaves: [32]

	1784	1788	1789
Whites	20,229	27,717	30,831
Free Colored	13,257	21,848	24,848
Slaves	297,079	405,528	434,429

The total population of St. Domingue in 1789 was nearly 520,000.

Whites	40,000
Free Colored	28,000
Slaves	450,000

Laborie, writing in 1798, after the colony had exploded, expressed the opinion that the Code Noir was framed too early, when experience with slavery was lacking. Emancipation was unrestricted, no limits were placed upon acquistion of property by the free colored population, there was no discrimination against them before the law. Restrictions were imposed later, but they were not very effective.[33] It is easier to prevent the growth of a wealthy and powerful group within a society than to degrade or destroy it once it has come into existence. The wealthy, educated *gens de couleur* defended their interests very well, and in the process, became the fuse which ignited the colony.

SOCIAL CONFLICT BETWEEN THE COLORED AND WHITE ELITE OF ST. DOMINGUE

The Haitian Revolution was precipitated by the response of the free colored population to attempts by whites to strip them of legal protection, to degrade them socially, and to destroy their network of influence with

[32] *Ibid.*, p. 1. The earlier figure for slaves was undercounted. Since slaves were subject to a head tax, the slave owners attempted to conceal the number of slaves they actually had. M. de Marbois, the last intendant, was more vigilant, and arrived at more accurate figures, but even these were considerably undercounted. P. J. Laborie, *The Coffee Planter of Saint Domingo* (London: T. Cadell and W. Davies, 1798), pp. 56, 57. The scale of concealment is shown in the example of the confiscation of 68 slaves from one master who concealed their existence from the census. *Loix*, Ordonnance de l'Intendant, June 19, 1756.

[33] Laborie, *Coffee Planter*, pp. 44–53.

persons and institutions that could offer protection, in order to dispossess them of coveted land, slaves, and other property. The system of racial discrimination was gradually built up over the years, and culminated with sharp discriminatory measures during the last two decades of the colony.

The basic conflict was over wealth and over power to protect the wealth. Because widespread intermarriage and more informal unions had resulted in the transferral of some of the best lands to the mulatto offspring of white planters, the economic struggle was also manifested in sexual rivalry. Julien Raimond, eloquent representative of the colored elite of St. Domingue in the French General Assembly, dated discrimination from shortly before the War of 1744, when the colony began to become prosperous and a large number of Europeans came over, including marriageable white women seeking to marry rich planters. But the virtues of the white women sent over in those days by the French government seemed "more than suspect, and their marriages with the whites did not have all the fruit that was anticipated." They were often passed over for more fertile *filles de couleur*, who also often possessed the added advantage of owning land and slaves. In spite of the presence of white women, white men continued to marry *filles de couleur* or to choose a woman from among their slaves "making them their wives, under the title of housekeepers." The daughters of the *gens de couleur* often married newly arrived white settlers. As the colony became more cultivated, the colored population grew rapidly at the expense of the white population, not only because of the lack of white women, but also because of the men's preference for colored women.

Many white families, coming over after the Peace of 1749, were jealous of the growing fortunes of the *gens de couleur*. After the Peace of 1763, there was a new wave of immigration. Educated *gens de couleur* returned from France where they had served in the House of the King, and as officers in various regiments; this provoked jealousy of their accomplishments from white settlers, who pushed for the passage of humiliating and oppressive laws. Several governors, including M. Dennery and M. de Bellecombe tried to control the hostile whites. But the result was a massacre; "at Martinique, on the day of Fête-Dieu, and in the other colonies, we saw the poor whites hunting down and murdering the *gens de couleur*, accusing them of imaginary plots." Marriage between white men and *filles*

145

de couleur was outlawed in 1768, but the situation did not change; the *filles de couleur* became concubines instead of wives. Many free colored landowners were deprived of their lands by "a host of tyrannical acts." But many held on to their property and slaves and maintained a strong position.[34]

The first right which came under attack was access to political positions, because political power is the ultimate arbiter of economic power, and denial of political rights was a precondition for withdrawing the free colored population from access to public protection. In 1706, a mulatto was appointed procureur du roi, in spite of the protest of the *Doyen du Conseil* that "a mulatto bastard cannot be received in any judiciary post."[35] By 1760, however, the king ordered that no *sang-mêlé* or white married to a *sang-mêlé* could hold office in the judiciary or in the militia, nor could he hold any other public employment in the colony.[36]

The impetus toward racial discrimination was not rooted in the French national character. "There is so little color prejudice in France," wrote Emilien Petit, 'that mulattoes, quadroons, and other descendants of the black race are received in the military corps reserved for the young nobility and as magistrates."[37] Racial discrimination in St. Domingue stemmed from the cold, calculated ambition and greed of the white colonists. There was a case where a free colored man was sold some property by a white man, who took the money for the purchase, then denounced him as a slave who could not prove he was free, had him legally reenslaved, and refused to deliver the property purchased because a slave was incapable of making a contract.[38] There was another case where a M. Boyer, a butcher in the neighborhood of Trou who was selling meat at $1\frac{1}{2}$ escalin per pound, had obtained from the government an exclusive monopoly for selling meat; this forced two free colored competitors who were selling the same quality of meat at 1 escalin per pound to close down. Since this privilege ate into the pocketbooks of all purchasers of meat, the monopoly

[34] Julien Raimond, *Observations sur l'origine et les progrès du préjugé des colons blancs contre les hommes de couleur* (Paris: January, 1791).

[35] *Loix*, Arrêt du Conseil du Cap, October 24, 1706.

[36] *Loix*, Arrêt du Conseil du Cap, May 22, 1760.

[37] Quoted in Lebeau, *Condition des gens de couleur libres.*

[38] *Loix*, Ordonnance des Administrateurs, February 26, 1770.

was finally set aside and the right of the free colored butchers to do business was protected.[39]

The list of discriminatory laws which flowered during the last three decades of the colony is long and ludicrous.[40] Racial discrimination became intense during the last few decades of the colony, not only as a means of controlling an ever-growing slave population, but even more important, as an instrument used by ambitious white colonists to degrade and dispossess a segment of the population which was vulnerable to attack on the grounds of ancestry. Whatever one might say in favor of the current emphasis upon a psychological explanation for the origin of race prejudice, the history of St. Domingue confirms Antoine Gisler's conclusion that "color prejudice, with its great repercussions, had largely a political origin . . . the fruit of the methodical effort of an entire century." [41]

Manipulation of Racial Conflict in the Face of the Independence Threat

The metropolis had no particular stake in the color of the planters of St. Domingue. As long as the French government and the French commercial interests continued to rake in countless wealth from the slave trade and from the refining and marketing of sugar, the conflict between the white and the colored elite of St. Domingue was a relatively small matter. Since the white elite had more influence at court, it succeeded in getting discriminatory measures passed. But the metropolis was not adverse to

[39] *Loix*, Ordonnance des Administrateurs touchant la Boucherie au Quartier du Trou, March 16, 1784.

[40] For a brief summary of some discriminatory laws, see James G. Leyburn, *The Haitian People* (New Haven: Yale University Press, 1941), pp. 18, 19. For texts of the laws, see *Loix*, Arrêt du Conseil du Cap, May 22, 1760; Ordonnance du Roi, April 30, 1764; Lettre du Ministre aux Administrateurs, September 25, 1774; Ordonnance du Roi, July 23, 1720; Ordonnance du Gouverneur Général, May 29, 1762; Lettre du Ministre à l'Intendant des Isles du Vent, December 30, 1741, cited in Gisler, *L'Esclavage aux antilles françaises*, p. 92; *Loix*, Arrêt du Règlement du Conseil du Port-au-Prince, September 24, 1761; Ordonnance du Juge de Police du Cap, April 17, 1762; Arrêt du Conseil du Cap, January 23, 1769; Arrêt du Conseil du Port-au-Prince, January 13, 1770; Lettre du Ministre aux Administrateurs, May 27, 1771; Règlement des Administrateurs, June 24 and July 16, 1773; Arrêt du Conseil du Port-au-Prince, January 9, 1778; Lettre du Ministre aux Administrateurs, March 13, 1778; Règlement provisoire des Administrateurs, February 9, 1779.

[41] Gisler, *L'Esclavage aux antilles françaises*, pp. 98, 99.

backing the colored elite in its struggle against the white elite if the interests of France demanded it.

The American Revolution raised the specter of a successful independence movement among the white planters of St. Domingue, and as part of its efforts to control the white planters, the metropolis, hoping to rely upon the loyalty of the colored elite as a weapon against independence-minded whites, seriously considered easing discrimination against the colored elite of St. Domingue. A memorandum dating from the 1780s communicated the views of His Majesty that today "the most thoughtful people consider the *gens de couleur* as the greatest barrier against troubles from the slaves. This class of men merit concern and care, and they lean toward tempering the established degradation and even bringing it to an end. This delicate subject demands profound thought, and should be carefully considered." [42]

Racial policies in the Spanish Empire were also liberalized during the rise of the independence movements in Latin America. The Crown adopted a policy of absorbing the ablest members of the free colored population, formally "whitening" them, in the hopes that they would remain loyal and present a counterweight to the independence-minded white creoles. A Consulta del Consejo de las Indias dating from 1806, citing the cooperation of the mulattoes with Miranda in Peru, explained this middle course. The privilege of being formally and legally whitened should not be so widely dispensed that it disrupts and disorganizes the public order, nor so restricted that it denies all hope for advancement, which would bring about equally serious consequences and weaken the fidelity and zeal for service to the king of some people who absolutely must be counted upon for the conservation of these dominions. Rather than grant full citizenship rights to all the colored people, individuals would be able to solicit "whiteness" from the king by virtue of their merits and outstanding service. [43]

The *castas* or free men of color were the decisive military force in the independence wars in Venezuela, and the acting captain-general of that colony urged the Crown to make concessions to them to win their loyalty to the Royalist cause. [44] The issuance of documents called *gracias al sacar*,

---

[42] Quoted in *ibid.*, p. 98.
[43] *DHFS*, vol. 3, pp. 821–28.
[44] James F. King, "A Royalist View of the Colored Castes in Venezuela, 1815," *Hispanic American Historical Review* 33, no. 4 (November, 1953):526–37.

formally "whitening" individual men of color who petitioned the Crown for this privilege, was accelerated during the independence wars, although the conditions set up were certainly difficult to qualify for. The party had to be the child of a legitimate marriage, from parents who had been born free, be married to a free woman, live in the Spanish dominions, and exercise a profession, trade, or useful occupation.[45]

Spain had to maintain a dizzy balance among conflicting forces in order to hold on to Cuba throughout the nineteenth century. In spite of sharp racist policies promoted for the benefit of plantation agriculture and internal security, Spain was not adverse to using the free colored and even the slave population as a threat over the heads of independence-minded Cuban whites, especially as annexationist pressures from the United States increased. By 1847, the free colored population had been thoroughly repressed. The greater danger to Spanish rule arose from annexationists from the United States allied with white Cuban creoles wishing independence from Spain. The same Captain-General O'Donnell, who had previously been warning of the danger to internal stability posed by the free colored population, quickly changed his tune.

The mulattoes and *pardos libres* have no sympathy with the *negro indígena*, and their mutual hatred is one of the conditions for maintaining the equilibrium of the Island, making it difficult for them to unite, making an uprising of consequence by the colored people impossible, the force of their numbers being nevertheless imposing enough to intimidate the whites in their projects against the legitimate government. But this happy equilibrium, maintained up to now, will shortly cease to exist if the growth of the slave population is not encouraged. A decrease in the slave population would lower the risks of conspiracies of the blacks, but facilitate those of the whites. Although the free Negroes offer no advantages for the development of agriculture, they should not be considered harmful, because they are generally employed in mechanical arts and trades, and maintain the equilibrium with the white population, which can thus easily be contained by the power of the government."[46]

[45] Fernando Ortiz, *La hampa afro-cubana: Los negros esclavos* (Havana: Ruiz y Cª, 1916), pp. 88, 89; James F. King, "The Colored Castes and American Representation in the Cortes of Cádiz," *Hispanic American Historical Review* 33, no. 1 (February, 1953):33–64.

[46] A.H.N. Ultramar, Legajo 3550, Expediente 16, No. 854, Carta de O'Donnell al Sec. de Estado, November 10, 1847.

The policy of favoring the African population as a means of keeping the *independistas* in check flowered during the 1850s, as annexationist pressures from the United States intensified. The colored militia and mutual aid societies were reestablished. Spain frustrated the filibustering expeditions from the United States by adopting a policy of Africanization of Cuba. Guided by the principle that Cuba would be Spanish or African, Spain threatened to encourage free black migration into Cuba from other West Indian Islands as well as migration of contract workers directly from Africa. In 1853, the Marqués de la Pezuela, who had made a reputation as an incorruptible administrator and an enemy of slavery while he had been governor of Puerto Rico, was appointed captain-general of Cuba.[47] Pezuela refused to take brides from the slave traders, took an interest in the material and moral conditions of the slaves, and ordered that all the *emancipados* should be set free. He attempted to set up a registry of plantation slaves, but the *hacendados* would not permit the authorities to enter the plantations, nor supervise the registration of the slaves. A united front of Spanish mercantile interests and Cuban planters forced the abandonment of the Africanization program within the first year of Pezuela's administration. He was thereafter speedily removed.[48]

José Antonio Saco interpreted Spanish defense of the illegal African slave trade as a means of intimidating Cuban creoles with the threat of slave uprisings, so they would continue to seek the protection of Spain. When the Cuban planters used their slaves for military purposes during the Ten Years War for Cuban independence, Saco could not restrain himself from gloating over the fact that the Spanish had been hoisted on their own petards.

Without taking into account the great differences which exist between Cuba and Spain's former continental colonies, she [Spain] believed that from one day to the other, Cuba would also proclaim her independence; and in order to prevent this, Spain winked at the entrance of blacks. The government looked upon them not so much as laborers for agriculture, but rather as instruments for political domination; a policy which could be

---

[47] Arthur F. Corwin, *Spain and the Abolition of Slavery in Cuba, 1817–1886* (Austin and London: University of Texas Press, 1967), p. 114. For a thorough discussion of this period, see Basil Rauch, *American Interests in Cuba: 1848–1855* (New York: Columbia University Press, 1948).

[48] Corwin, *Spain and Abolition of Slavery*, pp. 119–21.

very harmful to the cause of Spain, because it was easy for conspirators to take advantage of the same instruments, and obtain with them precisely what Spain was trying to avoid, as has unfortunately happened during the bloody insurrection which has just ended (1878).[49]

The study of racial policies in the two colonies under consideration would indicate that racism was intimately linked with, and stemmed from, the interests of social groupings in society which had something to gain from the degradation and dispossession of the black and colored populations, as well as from deliberate governmental policies directed toward ruling these colonies by manipulating conflict among the races.

[49] Saco, *Historia de la esclavitud*, vol. 3, p. 157.

EPILOGUE

THE DATA OF THIS STUDY indicate a very serious problem of social control in the slave plantation societies of Cuba and St. Domingue which became more acute as prosperity increased. Policy toward the slave population, toward religious conversion and education of slaves, toward slave law, toward emancipation, and toward the free colored population was determined by the urgent needs of the society, especially by the enormous problem of controlling the slaves. The legal and religious traditions, as well as the colonizers' preexisting attitudes toward race, appear to have been relatively insignificant in determining policy toward the African population, slave or free.

The key to understanding the contrasts between the slave system of the United States and that of the Caribbean and Latin America probably lies in variants in the emphasis upon enforced acculturation of the slaves to their inferior status in the social system for the sake of long-range social stability. The higher frequency of open rebellions and the higher degree of retention of obvious Africanisms in the Caribbean and in Latin America were not the result of the liberal racial attitudes of the Latin colonizers, but of the lack of concern about socializing a population which was looked upon as an expendable commodity to be quickly used up and then replaced. In colonies where there was a high rate of absentee ownership, less attention was paid to socializing the slaves because there was less concern from

152

absentee owners about the long-range stability of the colony. In St. Domingue, it was the colonial authorities who looked out after the long-range interests of the colony and clashed with the planters who had a get-rich-quick mentality. In nineteenth-century Cuba, the opposite was true. The stable creole planter class of Cuba favored an end to the African slave trade for the sake of internal stability, while government officials, allied with Spanish commercial interests, preferred to get rich quick by protecting the illegal African slave trade, regardless of the long-range interests of the colony.

In contrast, there was great concern in the English mainland colonies to promote social stability and minimize the danger of slave uprisings. African-born slaves were often seasoned or trained to function in the slave system in the British West Indies before being brought to the mainland. The planter class thought of itself as American and, especially after the American Revolution, of the United States as its permanent home. By the early nineteenth century, the African slave trade played a relatively minor role in replenishing the slave population. Slave-breeding, especially in the border states, was encouraged if not forced. The slave system enjoyed very favorable conditions for the procreation of an American-born slave population during the nineteenth century. Cotton, the major crop, was conducive to child labor. There was abundant land for the cultivation of food crops and the expansion of the slave system. Most of the slaves were American-born, forcibly acculturated from birth, and lived on small estates with their owners, allowing for more frequent contact between master and slave than was common on Caribbean slave plantations.

Any social system relies, in varying degrees, upon the carrot or the stick, upon manipulation or naked force. If the exploited can be convinced that they deserve to be exploited and that they are powerless to end their exploitation, the social order can be maintained with a minimum of strife. Because the slaves were looked upon as a necessary, permanent part of the population of the United States, racism was highly developed as a mind-control device designed to keep the slaves passive enough to insure the survival of the system, regardless of what the real relationship of forces might be at any given moment. This is the real answer to the question of why racism is, and has been, more powerful in the United States than elsewhere in the Americas. The apparent answer, the one most often given by historians, is that the slave system of the United States was unique in its cruelty and inhumanity. We have seen that this was not the case. The strength of racism in the United States is a reflection of the manipulativeness of the social system. But man is not infinitely manipulable. The zombies are coming out of the trance, the social system is coming unstuck, and there is no way to put it back together again. All we can do is to create something better.

BIBLIOGRAPHY

BOOKS

Aimes, Hubert H. S. *A History of Slavery in Cuba, 1511 to 1868.* New York: G. P. Putnam's Sons, 1907.

Bastien, Rémy. *Religion and Politics in Haiti.* Washington, D.C.: Institute for Cross-Cultural Research, 1966.

Boxer, C. R. *The Golden Age of Brazil.* Berkeley and Los Angeles: University of California Press, 1962.

Charlevoix, Père Pierre-François-Xavier de. *Histoire de l'Isle espagnole ou St. Domingue.* Paris, 1731.

Código penal vigente en las islas de Cuba y Puerto Rico. Madrid: Pedro Nuñez, 1886.

Collección de los fallos pronunciados por una Sección de la Comisión militar establecida en la ciudad de Matanzas para conocer de la causa de conspiración de la gente de color. Matanzas, 1844.

Corwin, Arthur F. *Spain and the Abolition of Slavery in Cuba, 1817–1886.* Austin and London: University of Texas Press, 1967.

Cuadro estatístico de la siempre fiel Isla de Cuba, correspondiente al año de 1846, formado bajo la dirección y protección del Escmo. Sr. Gobernador y Capitan-General Don Leopoldo O'Donnell, por una comisión de Oficiales y Empleados particulares. Havana: Impr. del Gobierno, 1847.

Curtin, Philip D. *Africa Remembered: Narratives by West Africans from the Era of the Slave Trade.* Madison: University of Wisconsin Press, 1969.

———. *The Atlantic Slave Trade: A Census.* Madison: University of Wisconsin Press, 1969.

Davis, David Brian. *The Problem of Slavery in Western Culture.* Ithaca: Cornell University Press, 1966.

155

Debien, Gabriel. *Plantations et esclaves à St. Domingue.* Dakar: Publications de la Section d'Histoire, Université de Dakar, 1962.

Deerr, Noel. *The History of Sugar.* 2 vols. London: Chapman and Hall, Ltd., 1950.

Donnan, Elizabeth (ed.) *Documents Illustrative of the History of the Slave Trade to America.* 4 vols. Washington, D.C.: Carnegie Institute, 1930–35.

Dutertre, Jean Baptiste. *Histoire générale des antilles habitées par les françois.* 4 vols. Paris, 1667–71.

Elkins, Stanley M. *Slavery: A Problem in American Institutional and Intellectual Life.* Chicago: University of Chicago Press, 1959.

Evans-Pritchard, E. E. *Witchcraft, Oracles and Magic among the Azande.* London: Oxford University Press, 1937.

Ferrer de Couto, Don José. *Los negros en sus diversos estados y condiciones; tales como son, como se supone que son, y como deben ser.* 2d ed. New York: Hallet Press, 1864.

Franco, José L. *La conspiración de Aponte.* Ser. 53. Havana: Publicaciones del Archivo Nacional, 1963.

Freyre, Gilberto. *The Mansions and the Shanties.* New York: Alfred A. Knopf, 1963.

———. *The Masters and the Slave.* New York: Alfred A. Knopf, 1946.

Furtado, Celso. *The Economic Growth of Brazil: A Survey from Colonial to Modern Times.* Translated by Ricardo W. DeAguiar and Eric C. Drysdale. Berkeley and Los Angeles: University of California Press, 1963.

Gaston-Martin, *Histoire de l'esclavage dans les colonies françaises.* Paris: Presses Universitaires de France, 1948.

Gelfand, Michael. *The African Witch.* Edinburgh and London: E. and S. Livingstone, Ltd., 1967.

Gisler, Antoine. *L'Esclavage aux antilles françaises (XVIIe–XIXe siècles): Contribution au problème de l'esclavage.* Fribourg: Editions Universitaires Fribourg Suisse, 1964.

Gonzalez del Valle y Ramirez, Francisco. *La Conspiración de la escalera.* Havana: Imprenta El Siglo XX, 1925.

Green, Lawrence G. *These Wonders to Behold.* Cape Town: The Standard Press Ltd., 1959.

Guerra y Sánchez, Ramiro. *La guerra de los diez años, 1868–1878.* Havana: Cultural S.A., 1950.

Harris, Marvin. *Patterns of Race in the Americas.* New York: Walker, 1964.

Hartz, Louis. *The Founding of New Societies.* New York: Harcourt, Brace and World, Inc., 1964.

Herskovits, Melville J. *Dahomey, An Ancient West African Kingdom.* 2 vols. New York: J. J. Augustin, 1928.

———. *Life in a Haitian Valley.* New York: Alfred A. Knopf, 1937.

———. *The New World Negro: Selected Papers in Afroamerican Studies.*

Edited by Frances S. Herskovits. Bloomington: Indiana University Press, 1966.

————, and Frances S. *Dahomean Narrative: A Cross-Cultural Analysis.* Evanston: Northwestern University Press, 1958.

————. *Rebel Destiny: Among the Bush Negroes of Dutch Guiana.* New York and London: McGraw-Hill, 1934.

Hilliard d'Auberteuil. *Considérations sur l'état présent de la colonie française de St. Domingue.* 2 vols. Paris, 1776–77.

Humboldt, Alexander von. *The Island of Cuba.* New York: Derby and Jackson, 1856.

Humboldt, Baron de. *Ensayo político sobre la isla de Cuba.* Havana: Publicación del Archivo Nacional de Cuba, 1960.

James, C. L. R. *The Black Jacobins.* 2d ed. rev. New York: Vintage Books, 1963.

Klein, Herbert S. *Slavery in the Americas: A Comparative Study of Virginia and Cuba.* Chicago: University of Chicago Press, 1967.

Konetzke, Richard, ed. *Colección de documentos para la historia de la formación social de Hispanoamérica, 1493–1810.* 3 vols. Madrid, 1962.

Korngold, Ralph. *Citizen Toussaint.* Boston: Little, Brown and Co., 1944.

Labat, Père Jean-Baptiste. *Nouveau voyage aux isles de l'Amérique.* 2 vols. Paris: Editions Duchartre, 1931.

Laborie, P. J. *The Coffee Planter of Saint Domingo with an Appendix, Containing a View of the Constitution, Government, Laws, and State of that Colony Previous to the Year 1789.* London: T. Cadell and W. Davies, 1798.

Laing, R. D. *The Politics of the Family.* Toronto: C.B.C. Publications, 1969.

Lebeau, Auguste. *De la condition des gens de couleur libres sous l'Ancien Régime d'après des documents des archives coloniales.* Paris: Guillaumin et Cᵢᵉ, 1903.

Leyburn, James G. *The Haitian People.* New Haven: Yale University Press, 1941.

Ligon, Richard. *A True and Exact History of the Island of Barbados.* London, 1757.

Macinnes, C. M. *England and Slavery.* Bristol: J. W. Arrowsmith Ltd., 1934.

Madden, Richard R. *The Island of Cuba.* London, 1853.

Mannix, Daniel Pratt, in collaboration with Malcolm Cowley. *Black Cargoes: A History of the Atlantic Slave Trade.* New York: Viking Press, 1962.

Mellafe, Rolondo. *La esclavitud en Hispanoamérica.* Buenos Aires: Eudeba Editorial Universitaria de Buenos Aires, 1964.

Montejo, Esteban. *The Autobiography of a Runaway Slave.* Edited by Miguel Barnet, and translated by Jocasta Innes. New York: Random House, 1968.

Moreau de St.-Méry, M. L. E. *Description topographique, physique, civile, politique, et historique de la partie française de l'Isle Saint-Domingue.* 4 vols. Philadelphia, 1797.

———. *Description topographique, physique, civile, politique, et historique de la partie française de l'Isle St. Domingue.* 4 vols. Paris: Librarie Larose, 1958.

———. *Loix et constitutions des colonies françaises de l'Amérique sous le vent.* 6 vols. Paris, 1784–89.

Moreno Fraginals, Manuel. *El ingenio: El complejo económico social cubano del azúcar.* Havana: Comisión Nacional Cubana de la UNESCO, 1964.

Mörner, Magnus. *Race Mixture in the History of Latin America.* Boston: Little, Brown and Co., 1967.

Newton, Arthur P. *The European Nations in the West Indies: 1493–1688.* London: A. and C. Black Ltd., 1933.

Nieuhoff, Johan. *Voyages and Travels into Brazil and the East Indies, 1643.* Extracted from Awsham Churchill, *A Collection of Voyages and Travels,* vol. 2. London, 1704.

Ortiz, Fernando. *Cuban Counterpoint: Tobacco and Sugar.* Translated by Harriet de Onís. New York: Alfred A. Knopf, 1947.

———. *La hampa afro-cubano: Los negros esclavos.* Havana: Ruiz y Cª, 1916.

Parrinder, Geoffrey. *African Traditional Religion.* London: Hutchinson's Universal Library, 1954.

———. *Witchcraft: European and African.* New York: Barnes and Noble, 1963.

Patterson, Orlando. *The Sociology of Slavery: An Analysis of the Origin, Development, and Structure of Negro Slave Society in Jamaica.* New York: Humanities Press, 1969.

Petit, Emilien. *Traité sur le gouvernement des esclaves.* 2 vols. Paris: Knapen, 1777.

Peytraud, Lucien. *L'Esclavage aux antilles françaises avant 1789.* Paris 1897.

Ragatz, Lowell J. *The Fall of the Planter Class in the British Caribbean: 1763–1833.* New York and London: The Century Co., 1928.

Raimond, Julien. *Observations sur l'origine et les progrès du préjugé des colons blancs contre les hommes de couleur.* Paris: January, 1791.

Rauch, Basil. *American Interests in Cuba: 1848–1855.* New York: Columbia University Press, 1948.

Recueil de diverses pièces et des discussions qui ont eu lieu aux Cortes générales sur l'abolition de la Traite et de l'esclavage des Nègres. Paris, 1814.

Saco, José Antonio. *Historia de la esclavitud de la raza africana en el Nuevo Mundo y en especial en los países américo-hispanos.* 4 vols. Havana: Cultural S. A., 1938.

Sandoval, Fernando B. *La industria del azúcar en Nueva España*. Mexico: U.N.A. de México, Instituto de Historia, 1951.

Scobie, Alastair. *Murder for Magic*. London: Cassell and Company, Ltd., 1965.

Stampp, Kenneth M. *The Peculiar Institution*. New York: Vintage Books, 1956.

Tannenbaum, Frank. *Slave and Citizen: The Negro in the Americas*. New York: Alfred A. Knopf, 1946.

Trayer, Paul. *Etude historique de la condition légale des esclaves dans les colonies françaises*. Paris, 1887.

Turnbull, David. *Travels in the West Indies*. London, 1840.

Vanufel, C., and Champion de Villeneuve. *Code des Colons de Saint-Domingue; Présentant l'Histoire et la legislation de l'ex-colonie; la loi de l'indemnité; avec les motifs et la discussion; les ordonnances royales relatives a son exécution; l'analyse du rapport fait au roi par la commission préparatoire; avec des notes explicatives*. Paris: MᵉVergne, 1826.

Verlinden, Charles. *L'Esclavage dans l'Europe médiévale*. Brugge: De Tempel, 1955.

Williams, Eric. *Capitalism and Slavery*. Chapel Hill: University of North Carolina Press, 1944.

Wilson, Monica. *Good Company: A Study of Nyakyusa Age Villages*. Boston: Beacon Press, 1963.

Woodson, Carter G. *The Negro in Our History*. Washington, D.C.: The Associated Publishers, Inc., 1947.

Wurdemann, J. G. F. *Notes on Cuba*. Boston: James Monroe and Co., 1844.

Zaragoza, Justo. *Las insurrecciones de Cuba. Apuntes para la historia política de esta isla en el presente siglo*. 2 vols. Madrid: Imp. de M. G. Hernàndez, 1872–73.

ARTICLES AND PERIODICALS

Carranca y Trujillo, Raúl. "El estatuo jurídico de los esclavos en las postrimerías de la colonización español." *Revista de Historia de América* 1, no. 3 (September, 1938):20–60.

Goveia, Elsa V. Comment on Herbert S. Klein's "Anglicanism, Catholicism and the Negro Slave." *Comparative Studies in Society and History* 8, no. 3 (April, 1966):325–27.

———. "Influence of Religion in the West Indies." *History of Religion in the New World, The Americas* 14, no. 4 (April, 1958):174–80.

———. "The West Indian Slave Laws of the Eighteenth Century." *Revista de ciencias sociales* 4 (March, 1960):75–105.

Hall, Gwendolyn Midlo. "Negro Slaves in the Americas." *Freedomways* 4, no. 3 (Summer, 1964):296–327.

Hernández y Sánchez-Barba, Mario. "David Turnbull y el problema de la esclavitud en Cuba." *Anuario de Estudios Americanos*, vol. 14 (1957), pp. 241–99.

Jordan, Winthrop D. "American Chiaroscuro: The Status and Definition of Mulattoes in the British Colonies." *William and Mary Quarterly* 19, no. 2 (April, 1962):183–200.

King, James F. "A Royalist View of the Colored Castes in Venezuela, 1815." *Hispanic American Historical Review* 33, no. 4 (November, 1953):526–37.

————. "The Colored Castes and American Representation in the Cortes of Cádiz." *Hispanic American Historical Review* 33, no. 1 (February, 1953):33–64.

Malagón, Javier, "Un documento del siglo XVIII para la historia de la esclavitud en las Antilles." *Imago Mundo* 1, no. 2 (September, 1955): 38–56.

Mintz, Sidney W. Introduction to *Sugar and Society in the Caribbean: An Economic History of Cuban Arigrculture*, by Ramiro Guerra y Sanchez and translated by Marjory M. Urquidi. New Haven: Yale University Press, 1964.

————. "Labor and Sugar in Puerto Rico and Jamaica." *Camparative Studies in Society and History* 1, no. 3 (March, 1959):273–83.

Sio, Arnold. "Interpretation of Slavery: The Slave Status in the Americas." *Comparative Studies in Society and History* 7, no. 3 (April, 1965): 289–308.

Wallace, Anthony F. C. "Revitalization Movements." *American Anthropologist* 58, no. 2 (April, 1956):164–81.

Zavala, Silvio, "Los trabajadores antillaños en el siglo XVI." *Revista de Historia de América* 1, no. 3 (September, 1938):60–89.

INDEX

161

166